WILD WEATHER

Storms, Meteorology, and Climate

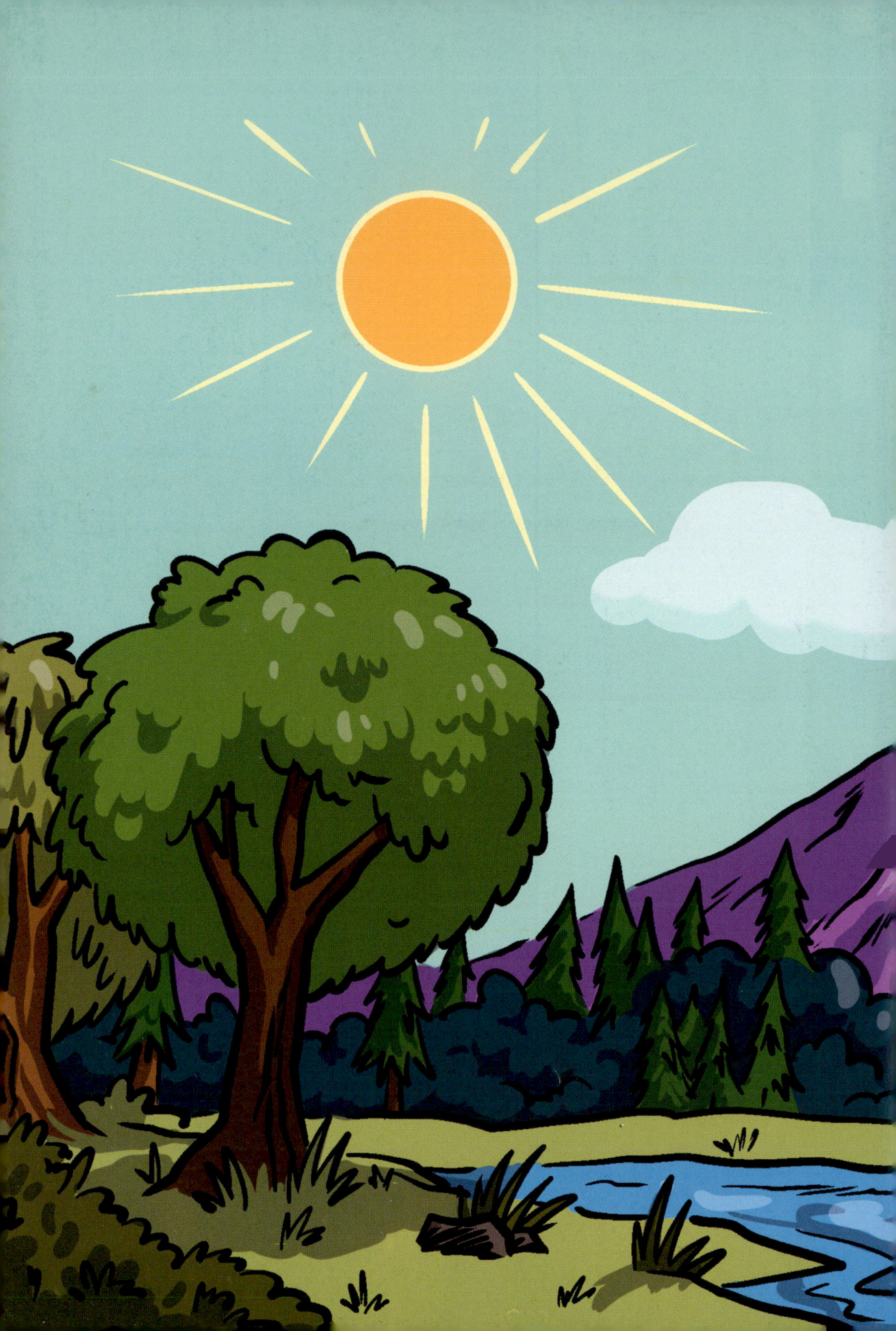

WILD WEATHER

Storms, Meteorology, and Climate

written by
MK REED

illustrated by
JONATHAN HILL

with color by
NYSSA ORU

:01

First Second

New York

To local news stations everywhere and in particular Matt Zaffino on KGW, the best meteorologist in the Portland Metro area.
—Jonathan

First Second

Text copyright © 2019 by MK Reed
Illustrations copyright © 2019 by Jonathan Hill

Don't miss your next favorite book from First Second! For the latest updates go to firstsecondnewsletter.com and sign up for our enewsletter.

Drawn in Clip Studio Paint EX with the Frenden brushes Red Real Pencil for the pencils and The Natural for the inks. Digitally colored in Procreate and Photoshop. Lettered in ComicCrazy.

Published by First Second
First Second is an imprint of Roaring Brook Press,
a division of Holtzbrinck Publishing Holdings Limited Partnership
120 Broadway, New York, NY 10271
All rights reserved

Library of Congress Control Number: 2018938084

Paperback ISBN: 978-1-62672-790-8
Hardcover ISBN: 978-1-62672-789-2

Our books may be purchased in bulk for promotional, educational, or business use. Please contact your local bookseller or the Macmillan Corporate and Premium Sales Department at (800) 221-7945 ext. 5442 or by e-mail at MacmillanSpecialMarkets@macmillan.com.

First edition, 2019
Edited by Dave Roman
Book design by John Green
Meteorology consultant: Alicia Wasula

Printed in China by Toppan Leefung Printing Ltd., Dongguan City, Guangdong Province
Paperback: 10 9 8 7 6 5 4 3
Hardcover: 10 9 8 7 6 5 4 3 2

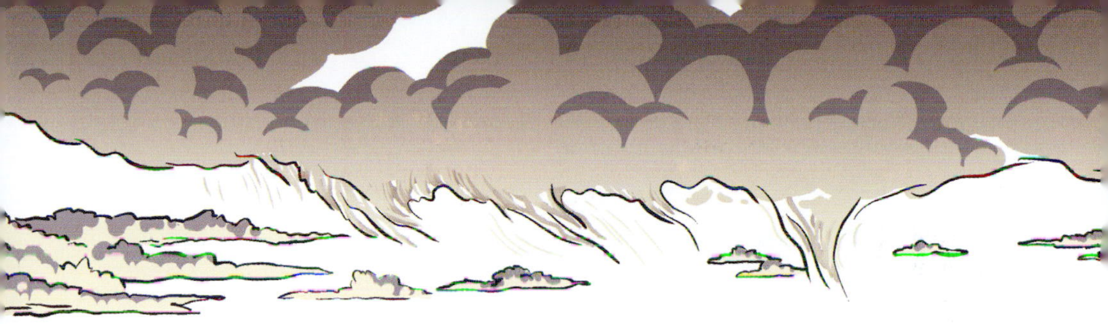

Weather can be amazing, exciting, fascinating, and terrifying . . . sometimes all at the same time! When the weather is nice and tranquil, you might not think too much about it. But when lightning darts across the sky or when high winds shake and rattle your house, weather may be the *only* thing you're thinking about.

I first realized the power of weather when I was seven years old, watching a TV show at home on a warm, humid spring night. Suddenly the broadcast was interrupted by a very serious-looking weathercaster. She pointed to a big blob on a radar and told us that our city was under a tornado warning. Was I scared? Absolutely. But I was also curious. How did this weathercaster know there was a tornado coming? And how did she stay so *calm*? I dashed across the house to let my parents know about the warning, and then I took a very quick look at those dark churning clouds. Right then, I knew I wanted to learn as much as I could about tornadoes. Before long, I was also interested in everything else about weather. I ended up studying meteorology in college and taking part in severe-storm research. So my life took a big turn on that dark and stormy night!

Most of my work these days involves writing about weather and climate, but I once got to spend a whole summer on the road as part of a research project, keeping an eye on the big thunderstorms of eastern Colorado (not in the mountains, but on the Great Plains). Our mission was to document what these storms were doing—raining, hailing, sometimes even producing twisters—and report back to the National Weather Service so they could fine-tune a new Doppler radar system. It was amazing to witness the power of the atmosphere day after day, but I also learned how challenging it can be to predict thunderstorms behavior and how difficult it can be to drive safely when you're surrounded by hazardous weather. Even trained professionals can get into

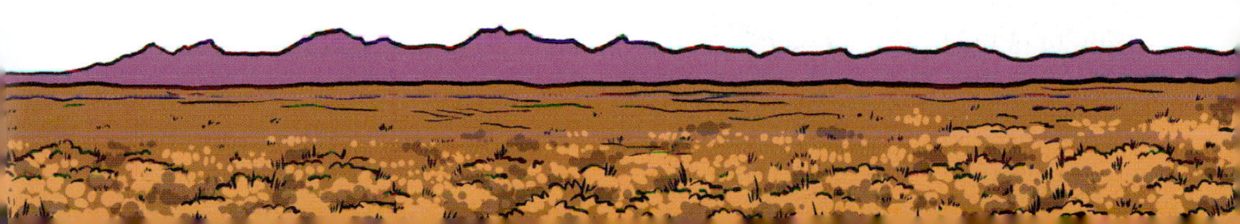

trouble when they chase storms, which is why it's best to watch the spectacular "sky shows" that nature gives us from a safe vantage point.

One of the great things about weather is it's free! The only equipment you *really* need to appreciate the atmosphere are your own senses. Even if you don't have a weather station, you can keep a "weather diary" and take note of what you see, hear, and feel every day. Sometimes the air feels like a soft, warm blanket—and sometimes it feels more like a thousand needles trying to pierce your skin. The wind can sound like a gentle whistle or a screaming blast. And there's an ever-changing parade of clouds, light, and texture in the sky above.

Even though weather is right in front of us all the time, the atmosphere can still feel mysterious. In this book, you'll find out many things scientists have learned about weather over the years: why we have seasons, why it rains and snows, what makes the wind blow, how hurricanes get named, why an EF5 tornado is so much worse than an EF1, and much more. Since hurricanes and tornadoes can be truly frightening, it's good that we have powerful tools, like radars and satellites, that keep track of wild weather from a safe distance. Forecasters at the National Weather Service and broadcast meteorologists like Stormin' Norman Weatherby—who you'll meet in this book—work hard to keep us informed about dangerous storms. Looking further out, we can now predict the weather days ahead of time with more and more skill, thanks to the help of computer programs that analyze the atmosphere and project it further into the future.

There's something else that many atmospheric scientists are examining: the impact of greenhouse gases on our weather and climate. Every time we burn coal, oil, or gas, we put heat-trapping gases into the air. These gases have now accumulated enough to raise global temperatures and to make heavy rains even heavier. What will our changing climate bring as your own lifetime

unfolds? What can we do to adjust to these changes? And how can we slow down the accumulation of greenhouse gases to help limit the changes to our atmosphere?

You can help! The world needs people with many different skills to analyze weather and climate and to keep everyone safe and well-informed. If you enjoy computing, you might help write the programs that track the atmosphere and predict what it will do next. If you like math and physics, you could become a research scientist, investigating one of the many yet-to-be-solved mysteries of our atmosphere. You might become an engineer, helping to design and build the next weather satellite. Do you enjoy teamwork? We need folks to organize big research projects all over the world and to help people transition toward cleaner energy. If you like to explain things, you could write articles to make weather and climate science easy to understand. You might even find yourself giving tomorrow's forecast on TV or on a smartphone, just like Stormin' Norman.

Weather is something you can enjoy and learn about your whole life. One man named Richard Hendrickson kept track of the weather on Long Island, New York, from age 18 until he was 101. That's more than 80 years! Thousands of volunteers like Richard collect weather observations every day and send them to the National Weather Service. Whether you're watching the sky as a scientist, a volunteer observer, or an everyday weather lover, I hope you find the atmosphere as exciting and awesome as I do.

—Robert Henson,
meteorologist and science writer,
coauthor of *Meteorology Today*,
and author of *The Thinking Person's Guide to Climate Change*

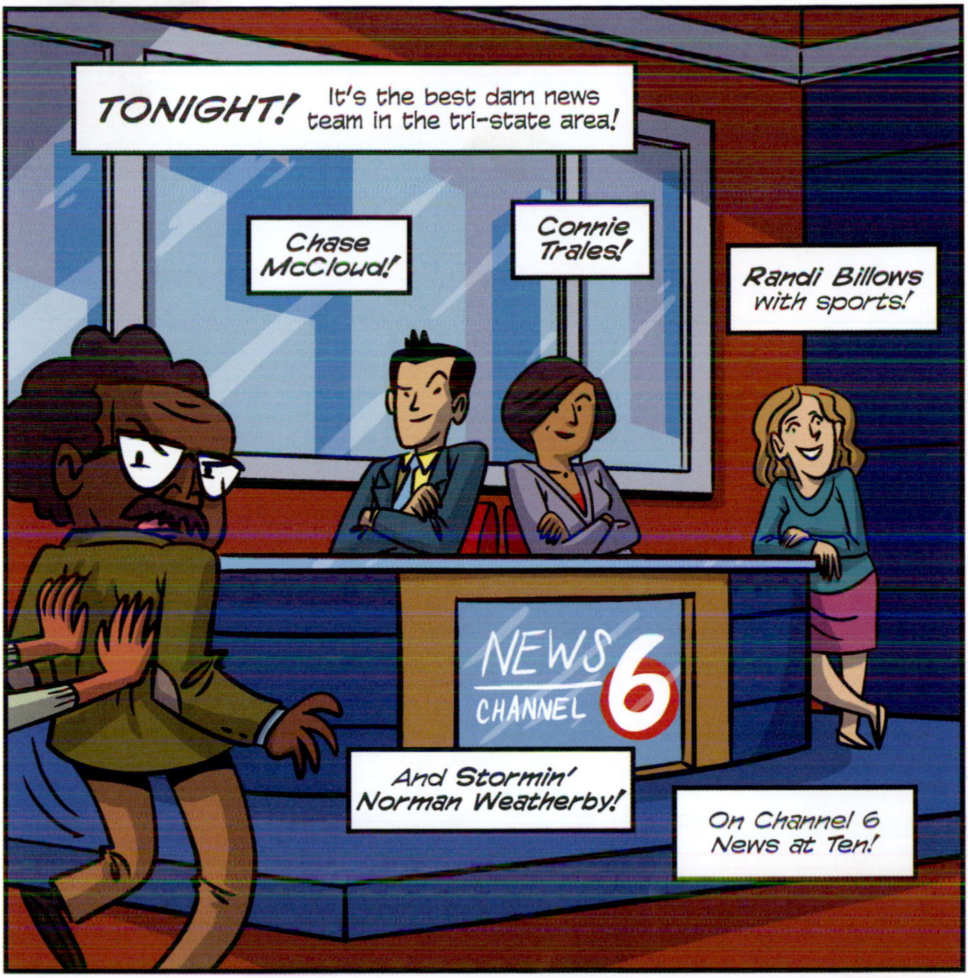
TONIGHT! It's the best darn news team in the tri-state area!
Chase McCloud!
Connie Trales!
Randi Billows with sports!
NEWS CHANNEL 6
And Stormin' Norman Weatherby!
On Channel 6 News at Ten!

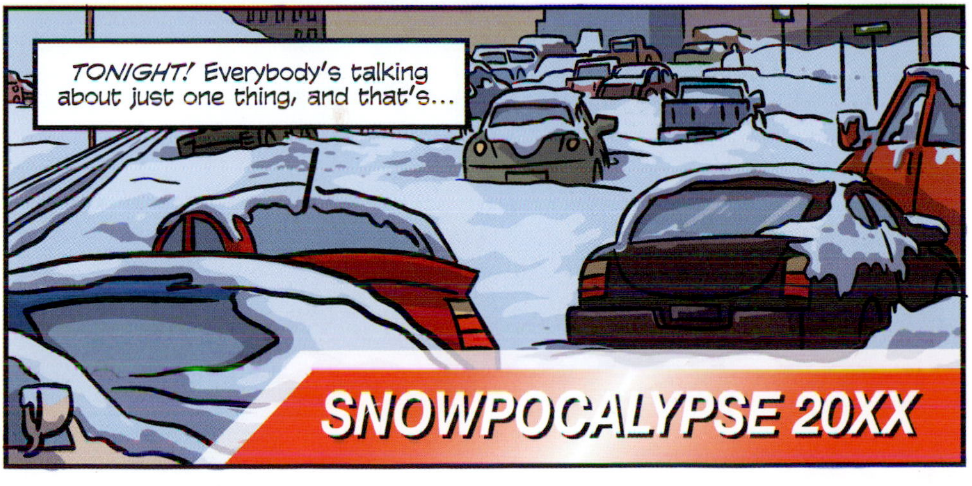
TONIGHT! Everybody's talking about just one thing, and that's...
SNOWPOCALYPSE 20XX

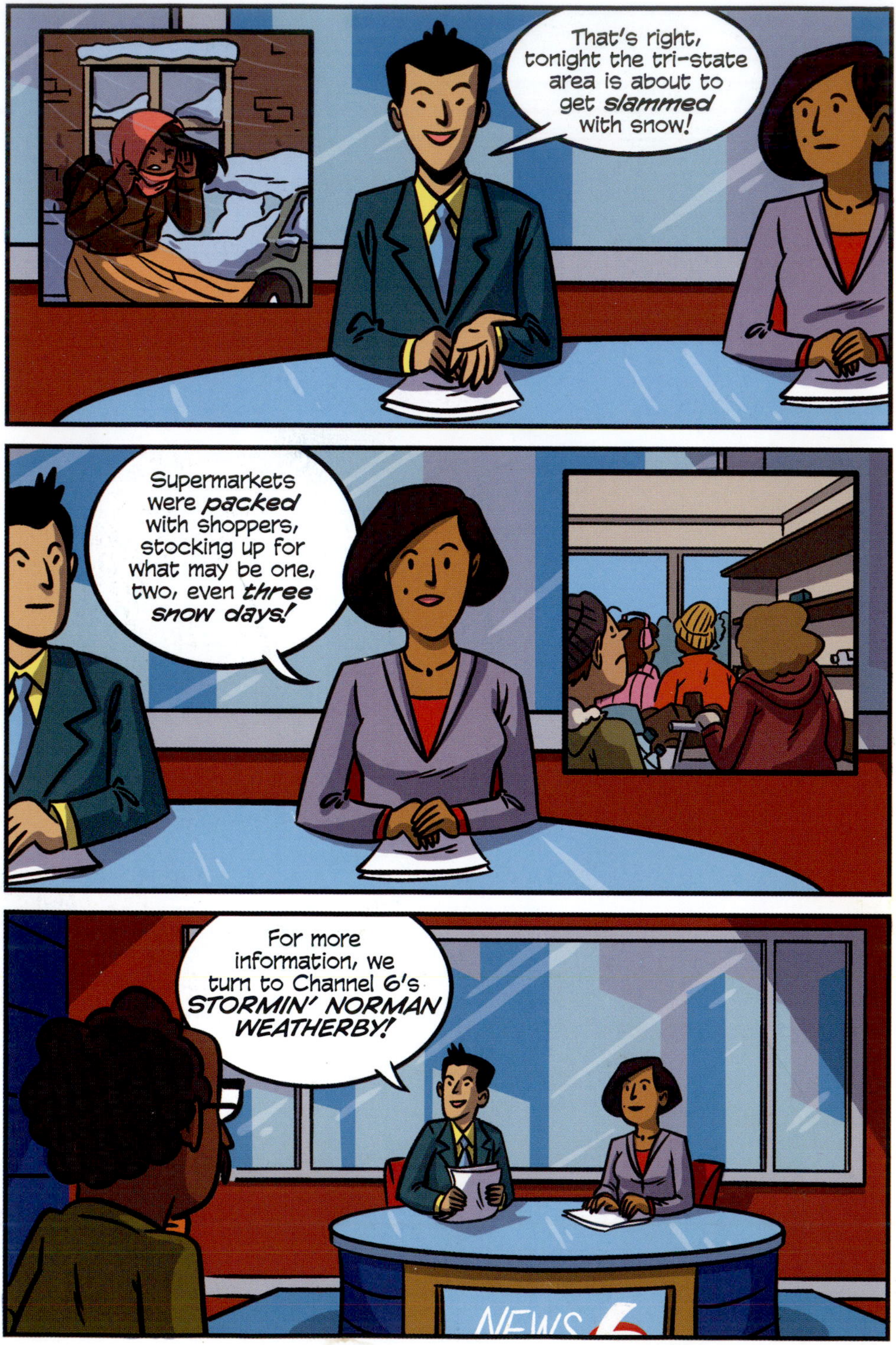
That's right, tonight the tri-state area is about to get *slammed* with snow!
Supermarkets were *packed* with shoppers, stocking up for what may be one, two, even *three snow days!*
For more information, we turn to Channel 6's *STORMIN' NORMAN WEATHERBY!*
NEWS 6

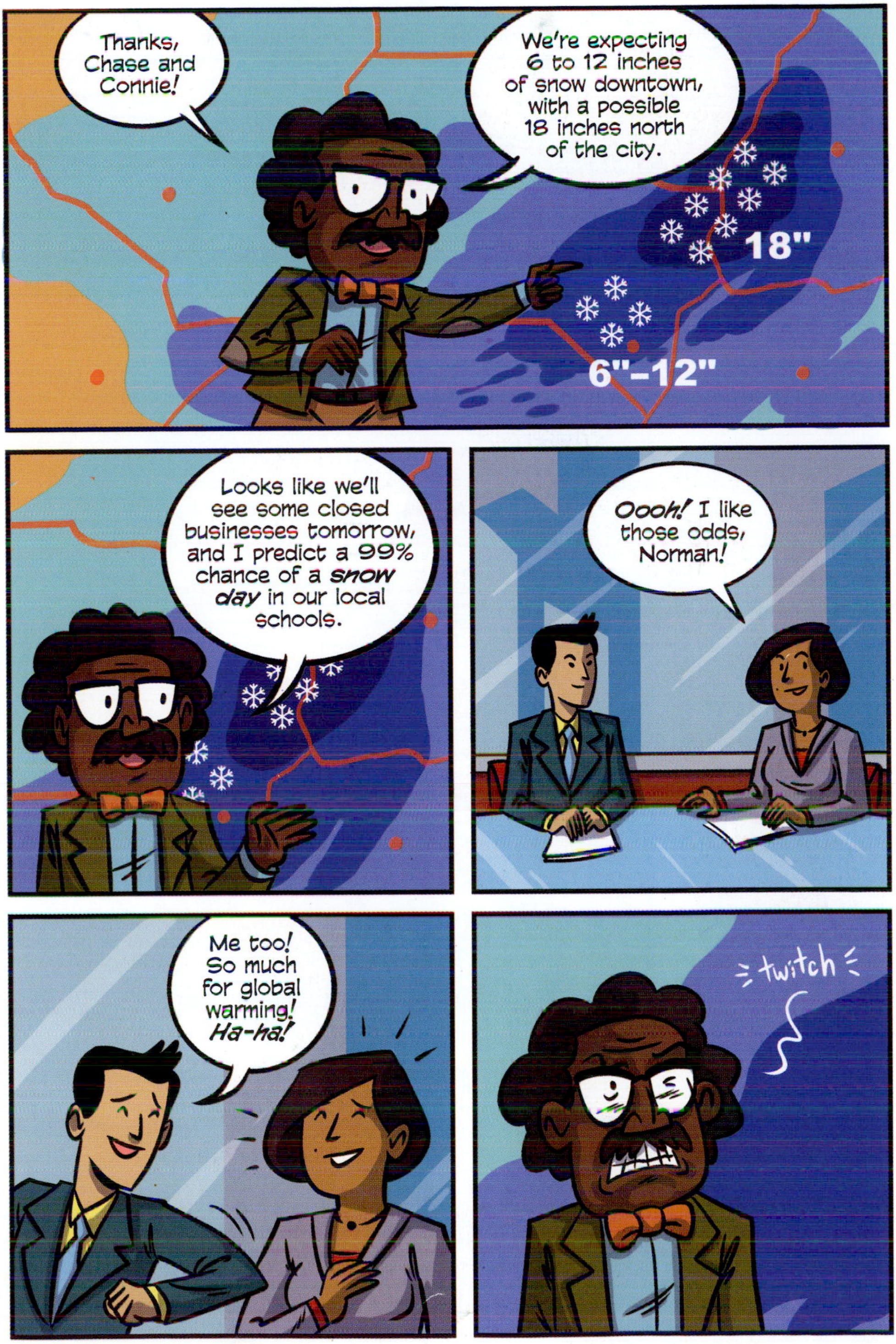
Thanks, Chase and Connie!
We're expecting 6 to 12 inches of snow downtown, with a possible 18 inches north of the city.
18"
6"-12"
Looks like we'll see some closed businesses tomorrow, and I predict a 99% chance of a *snow day* in our local schools.
Oooh! I like those odds, Norman!
Me too! So much for global warming! *Ha-ha!*
twitch

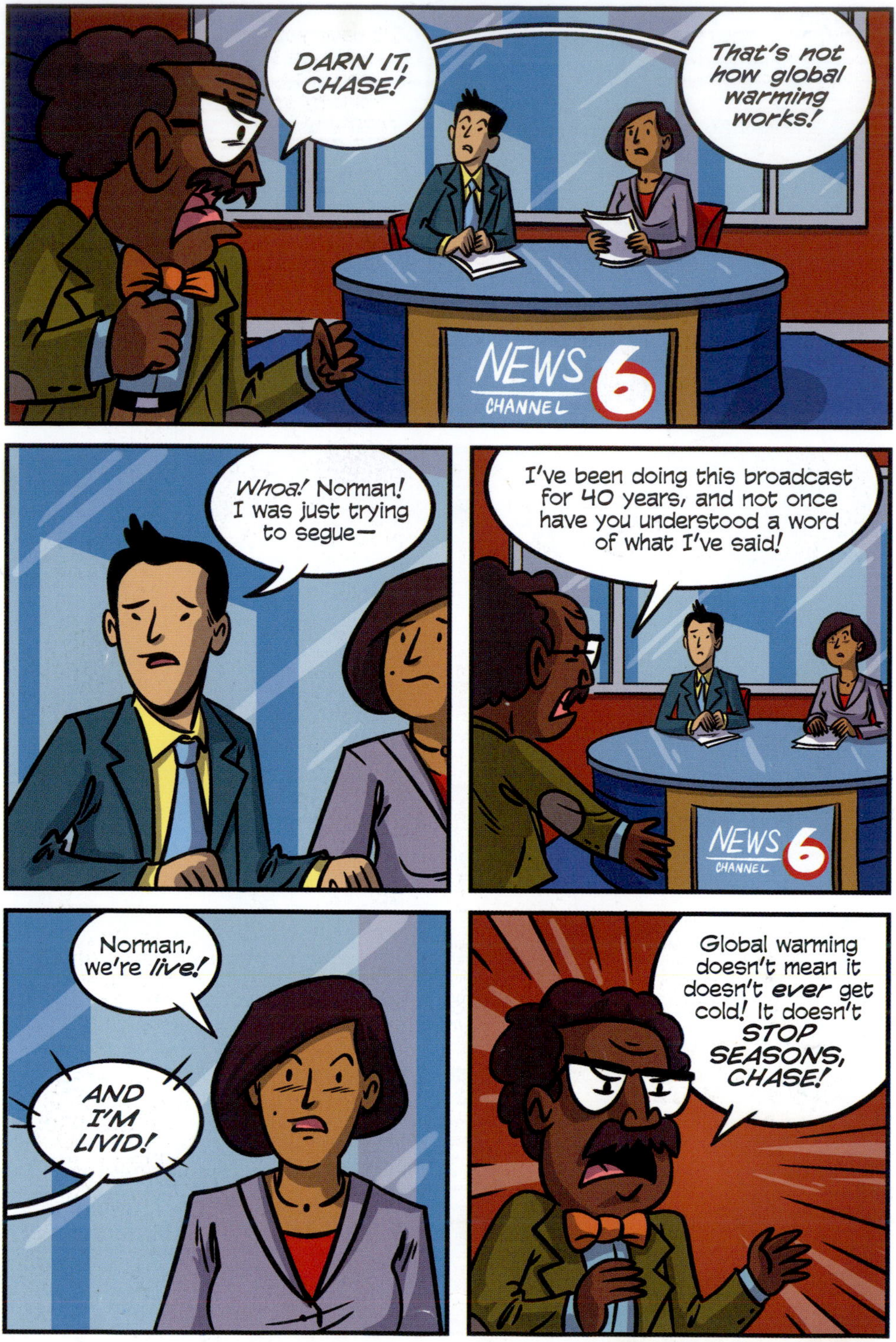
DARN IT, CHASE!
That's not how global warming works!
NEWS CHANNEL 6
Whoa! Norman! I was just trying to segue—
I've been doing this broadcast for 40 years, and not once have you understood a word of what I've said!
NEWS CHANNEL 6
Norman, we're live!
AND I'M LIVID!
Global warming doesn't mean it doesn't ever get cold! It doesn't STOP SEASONS, CHASE!

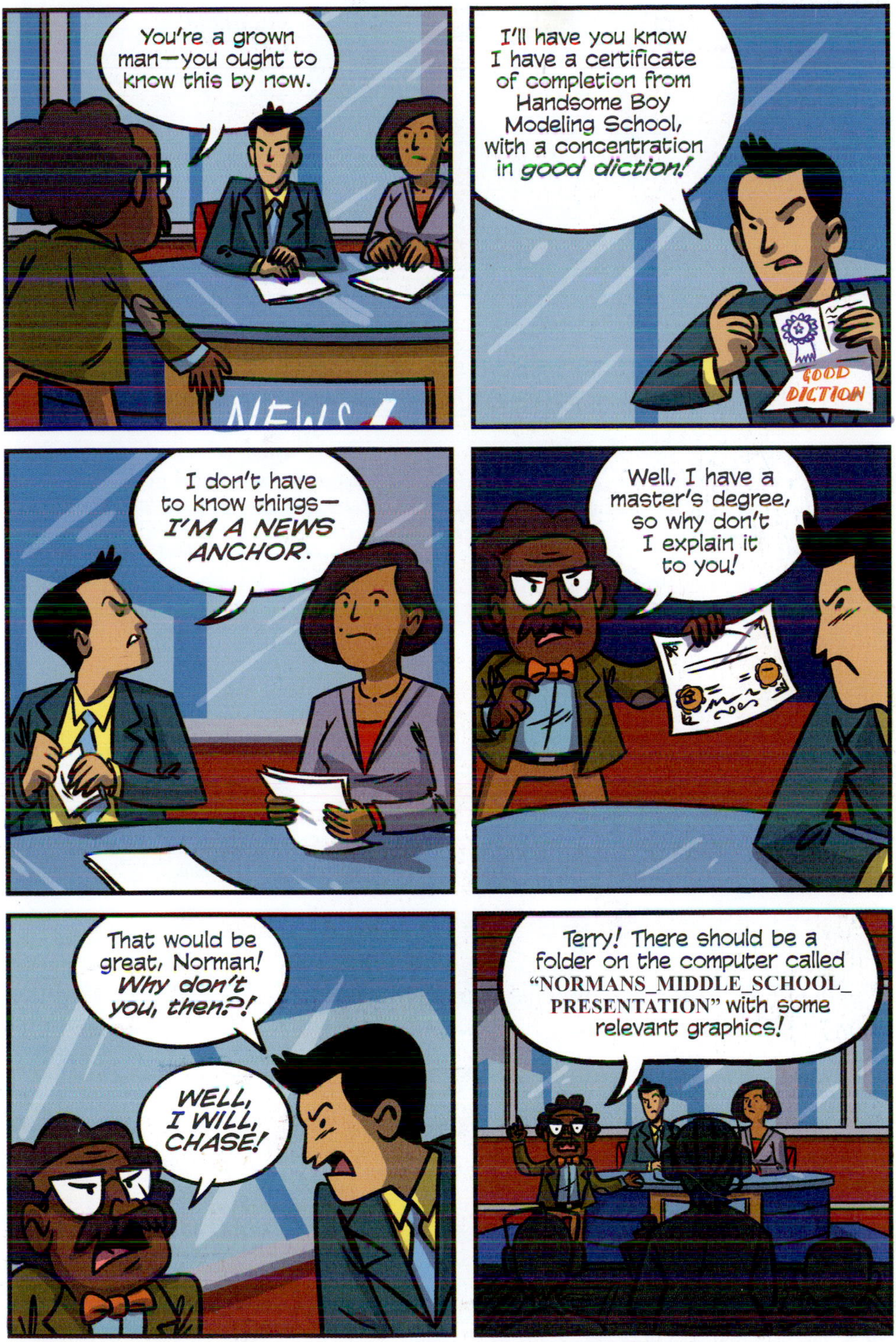

You're a grown man—you ought to know this by now.
I'll have you know I have a certificate of completion from Handsome Boy Modeling School, with a concentration in *good diction!*
GOOD DICTION
I don't have to know things—*I'M A NEWS ANCHOR.*
Well, I have a master's degree, so why don't I explain it to you!
That would be great, Norman! *Why don't you, then?!*
WELL, I WILL, CHASE!
Terry! There should be a folder on the computer called "NORMANS_MIDDLE_SCHOOL_PRESENTATION" with some relevant graphics!

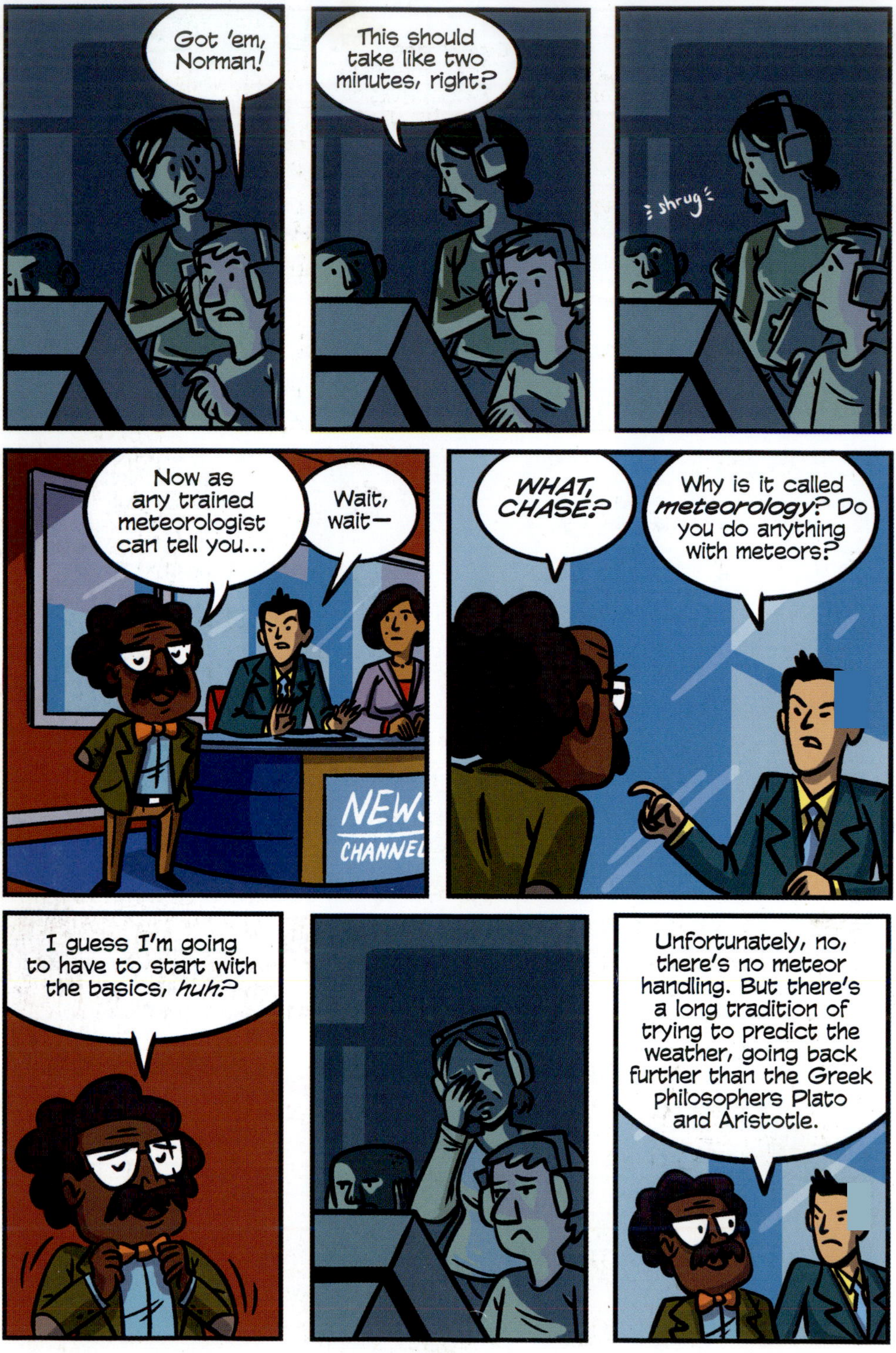
Got 'em, Norman!
This should take like two minutes, right?
shrug
Now as any trained meteorologist can tell you...
Wait, wait—
NEWS CHANNEL
WHAT, CHASE?
Why is it called *meteorology*? Do you do anything with meteors?
I guess I'm going to have to start with the basics, *huh?*
Unfortunately, no, there's no meteor handling. But there's a long tradition of trying to predict the weather, going back further than the Greek philosophers Plato and Aristotle.

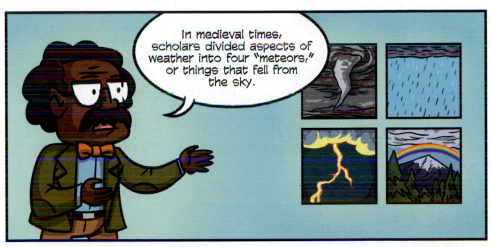

In medieval times, scholars divided aspects of weather into four "meteors," or things that fell from the sky.

Aerial meteors covered clouds and tornadoes.

Aqueous meteors covered rain, snow, hail, and other forms of precipitation.

Igneous meteors included lightning and meteorites.

And *luminous* meteors meant rainbows and halos, like St. Elmo's fire and the aurora borealis.

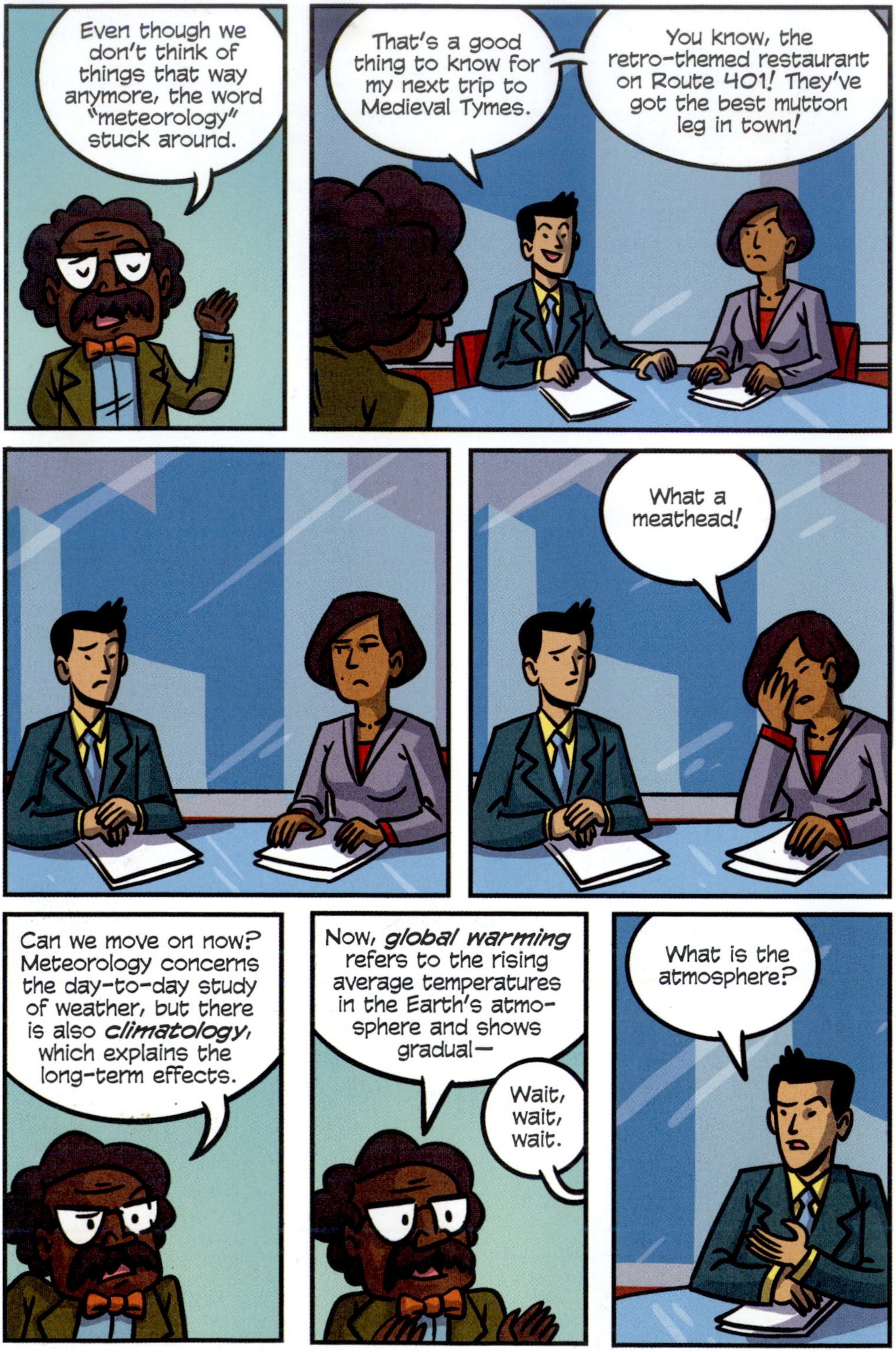
Even though we don't think of things that way anymore, the word "meteorology" stuck around.
That's a good thing to know for my next trip to Medieval Tymes.
You know, the retro-themed restaurant on Route 401! They've got the best mutton leg in town!
What a meathead!
Can we move on now? Meteorology concerns the day-to-day study of weather, but there is also *climatology*, which explains the long-term effects.
Now, *global warming* refers to the rising average temperatures in the Earth's atmo-sphere and shows gradual—
Wait, wait, wait.
What is the atmosphere?

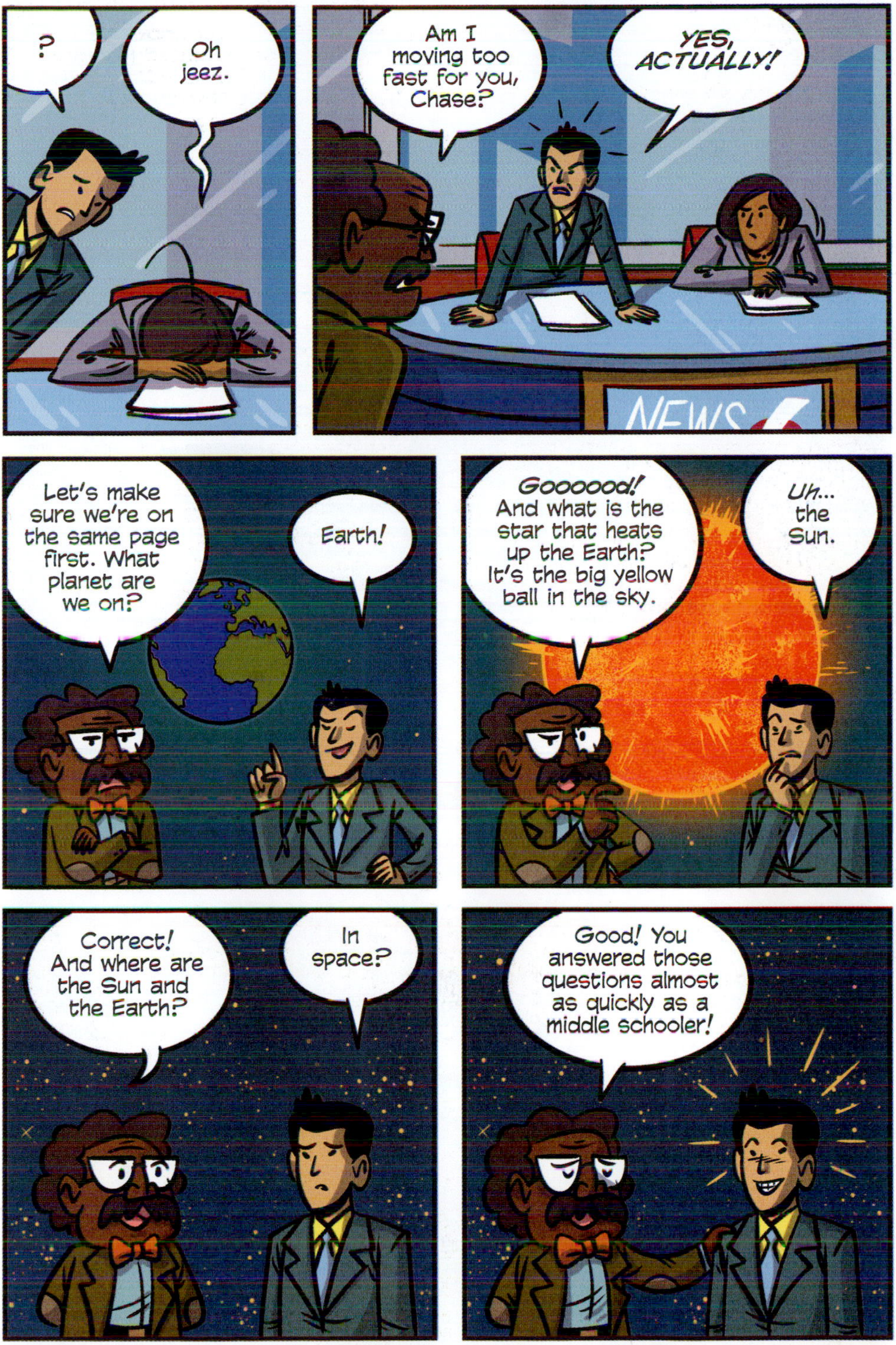
?
Oh jeez.
Am I moving too fast for you, Chase?
YES, ACTUALLY!
NEWS
Let's make sure we're on the same page first. What planet are we on?
Earth!
Goooood! And what is the star that heats up the Earth? It's the big yellow ball in the sky.
Uh... the Sun.
Correct! And where are the Sun and the Earth?
In space?
Good! You answered those questions almost as quickly as a middle schooler!

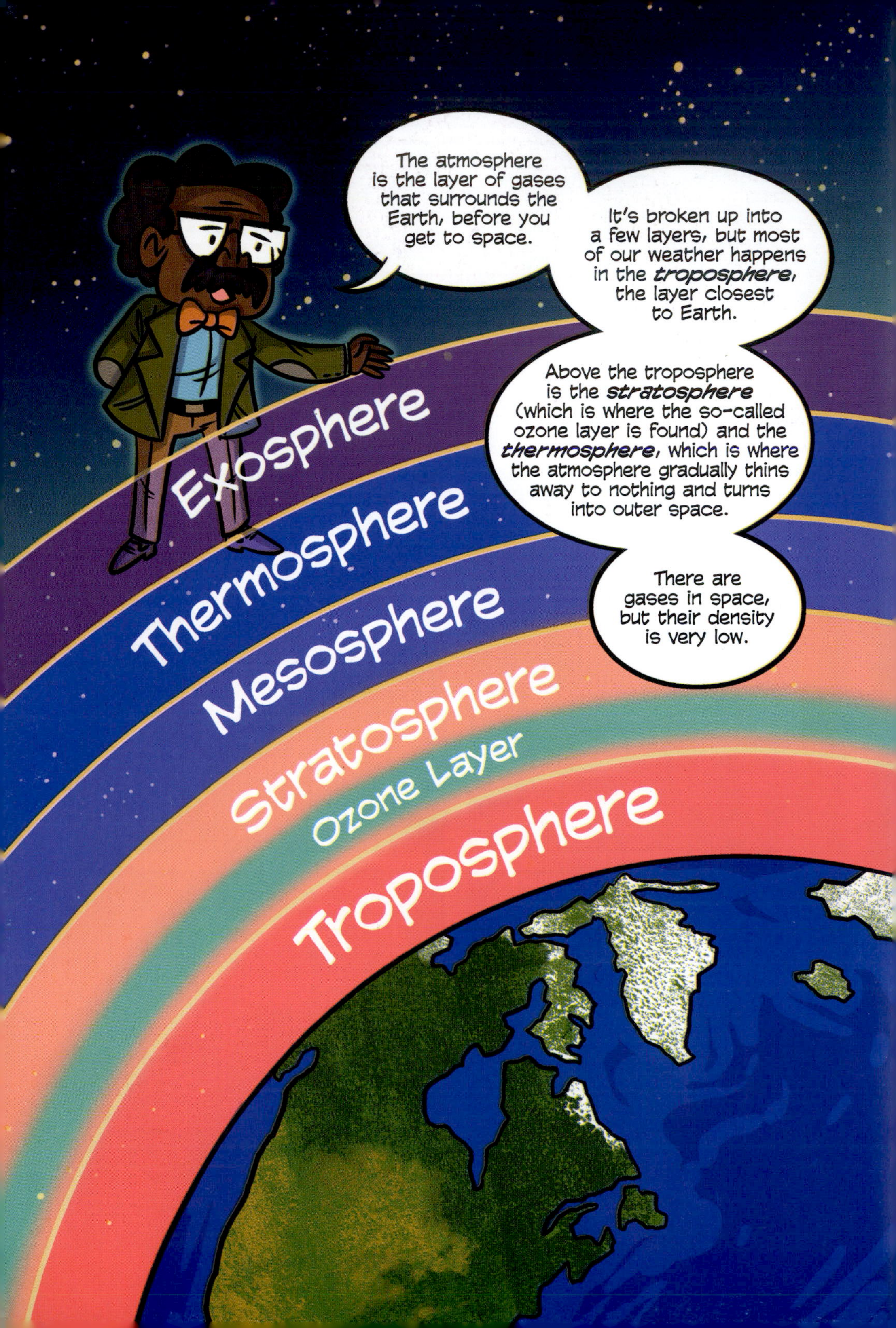
The atmosphere is the layer of gases that surrounds the Earth, before you get to space.
It's broken up into a few layers, but most of our weather happens in the *troposphere*, the layer closest to Earth.
Above the troposphere is the *stratosphere* (which is where the so-called ozone layer is found) and the *thermosphere*, which is where the atmosphere gradually thins away to nothing and turns into outer space.
There are gases in space, but their density is very low.
Exosphere
Thermosphere
Mesosphere
Stratosphere
Ozone Layer
Troposphere

Most of the air we breathe and exist in is within 10 miles of the Earth's crust.

Yes, and the crust is...?

Like the crust of a sandwich!

Well, really more like the outside of a bun or roll, Connie, but yes, it's the outermost layer of the Earth.

The other layers are the *mantle*, the *outer core*, and the *inner core*, but they don't have as much to do with weather.

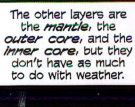

That's where volcanoes and earthquakes come from?

Well, yes, but it's a little more complicated than that.

While those would qualify as "natural disasters," they're more geology than meteorology.

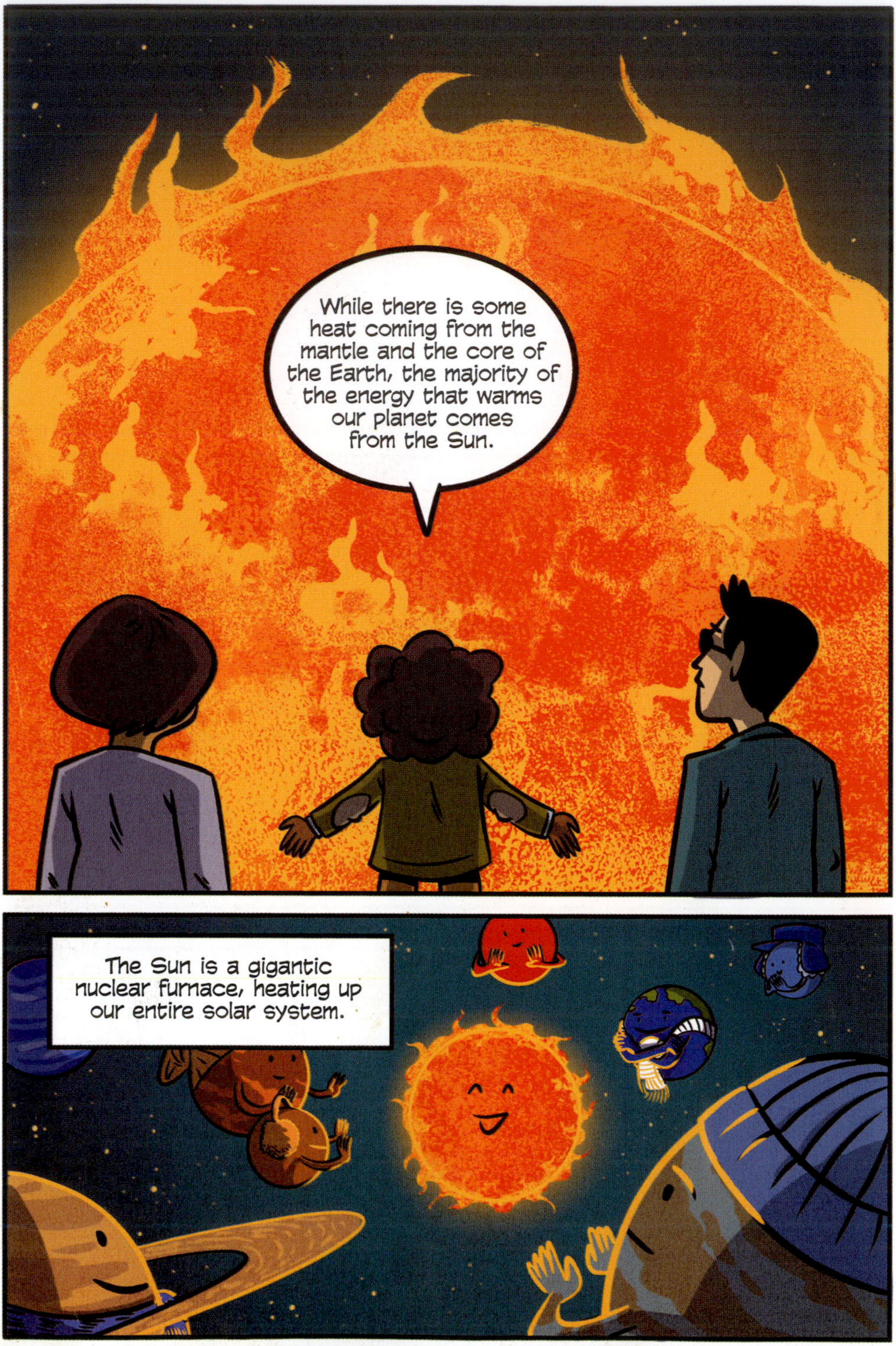
While there is some heat coming from the mantle and the core of the Earth, the majority of the energy that warms our planet comes from the Sun.
The Sun is a gigantic nuclear furnace, heating up our entire solar system.

The Sun's rays travel 93 million miles to Earth and enter the atmosphere.

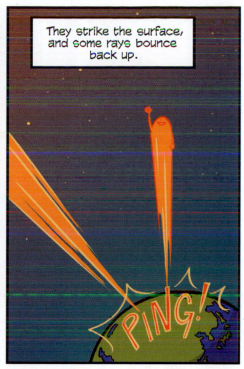

They strike the surface, and some rays bounce back up.

PING!

But the atmosphere traps the heat in.

Gotcha!

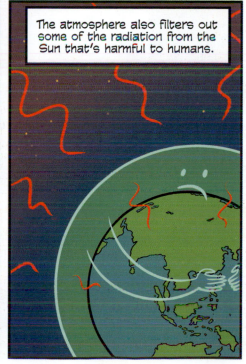

The atmosphere also filters out some of the radiation from the Sun that's harmful to humans.

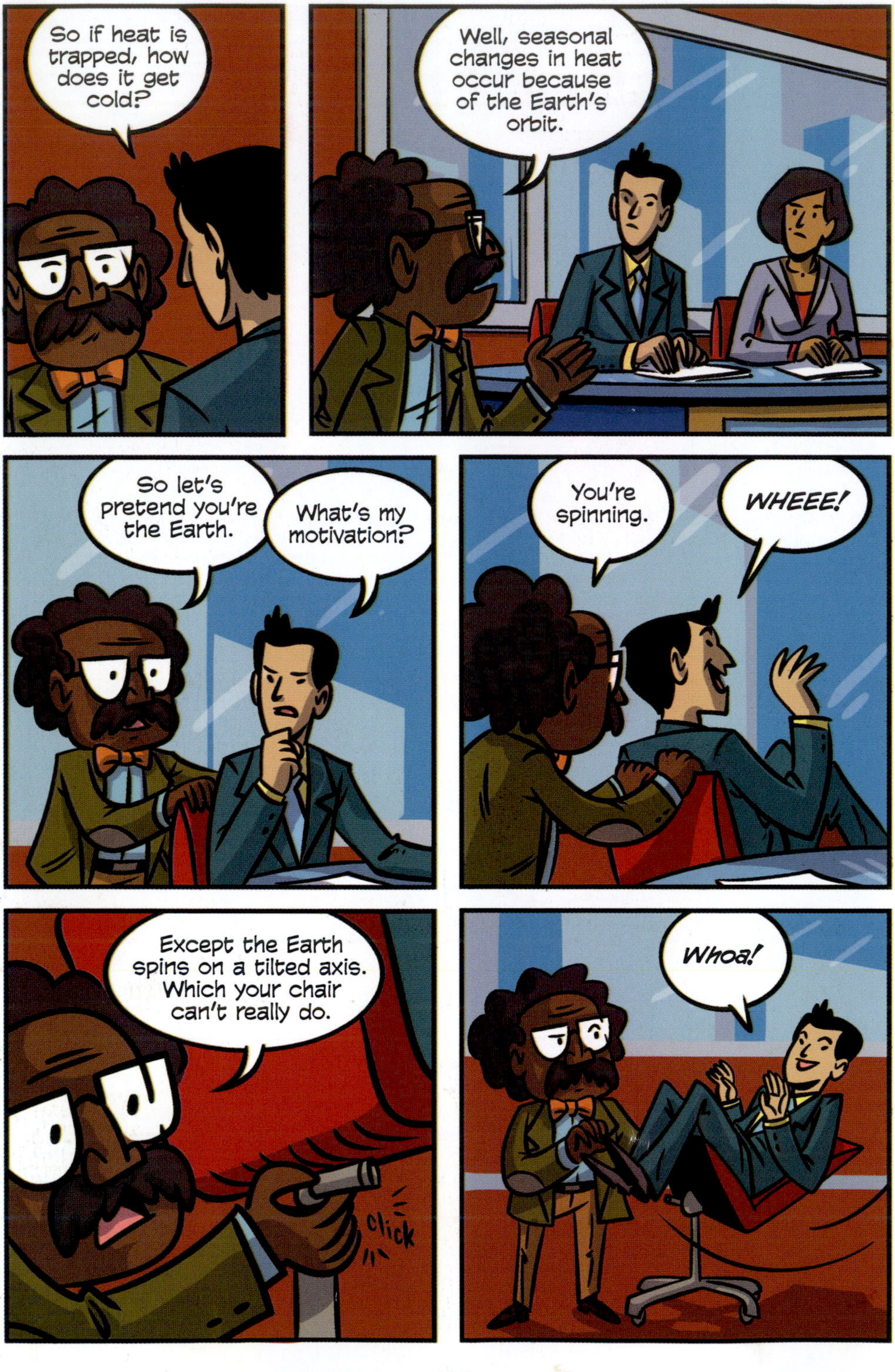
So if heat is trapped, how does it get cold?
Well, seasonal changes in heat occur because of the Earth's orbit.
So let's pretend you're the Earth.
What's my motivation?
You're spinning.
WHEEE!
Except the Earth spins on a tilted axis. Which your chair can't really do.
Click
Whoa!

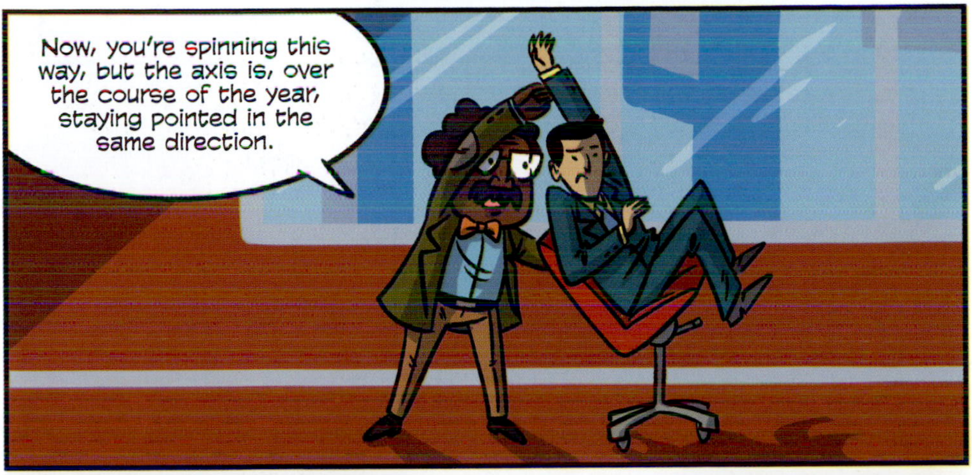
Now, you're spinning this way, but the axis is, over the course of the year, staying pointed in the same direction.

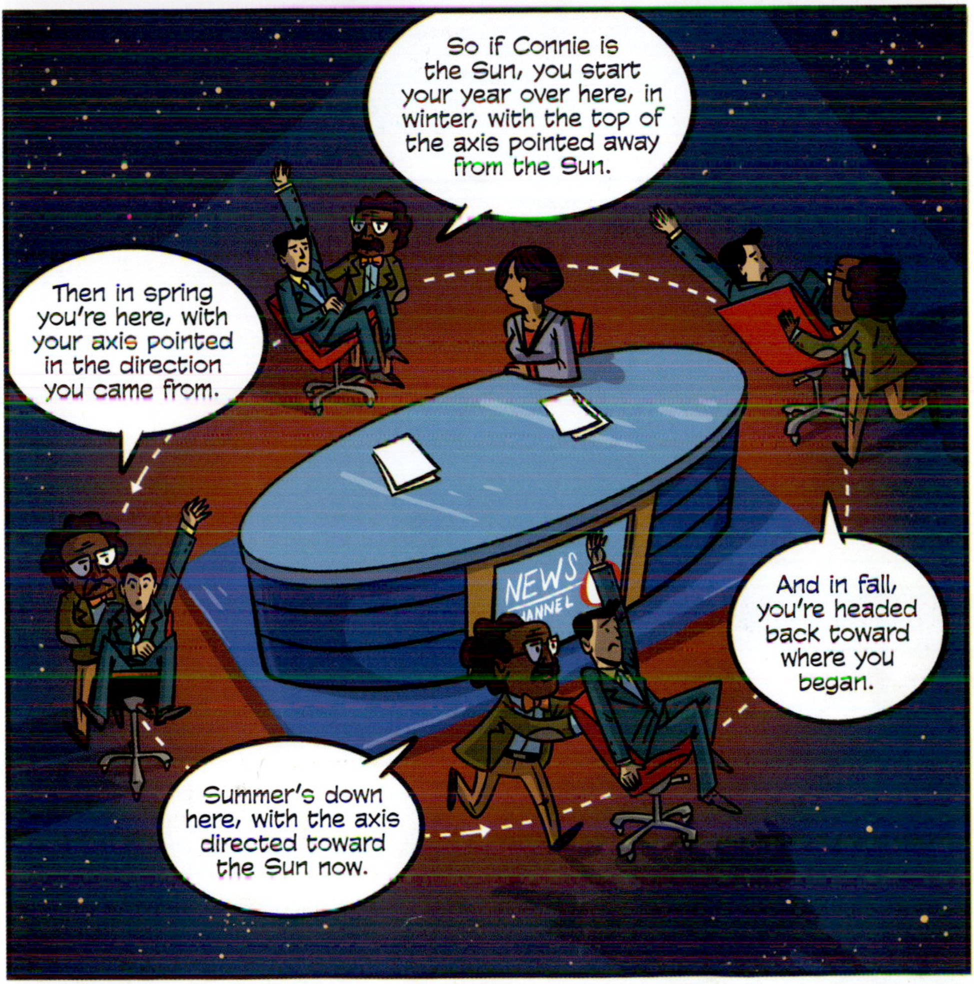
So if Connie is the Sun, you start your year over here, in winter, with the top of the axis pointed away from the Sun.
Then in spring you're here, with your axis pointed in the direction you came from.
Summer's down here, with the axis directed toward the Sun now.
And in fall, you're headed back toward where you began.
NEWS
CHANNEL

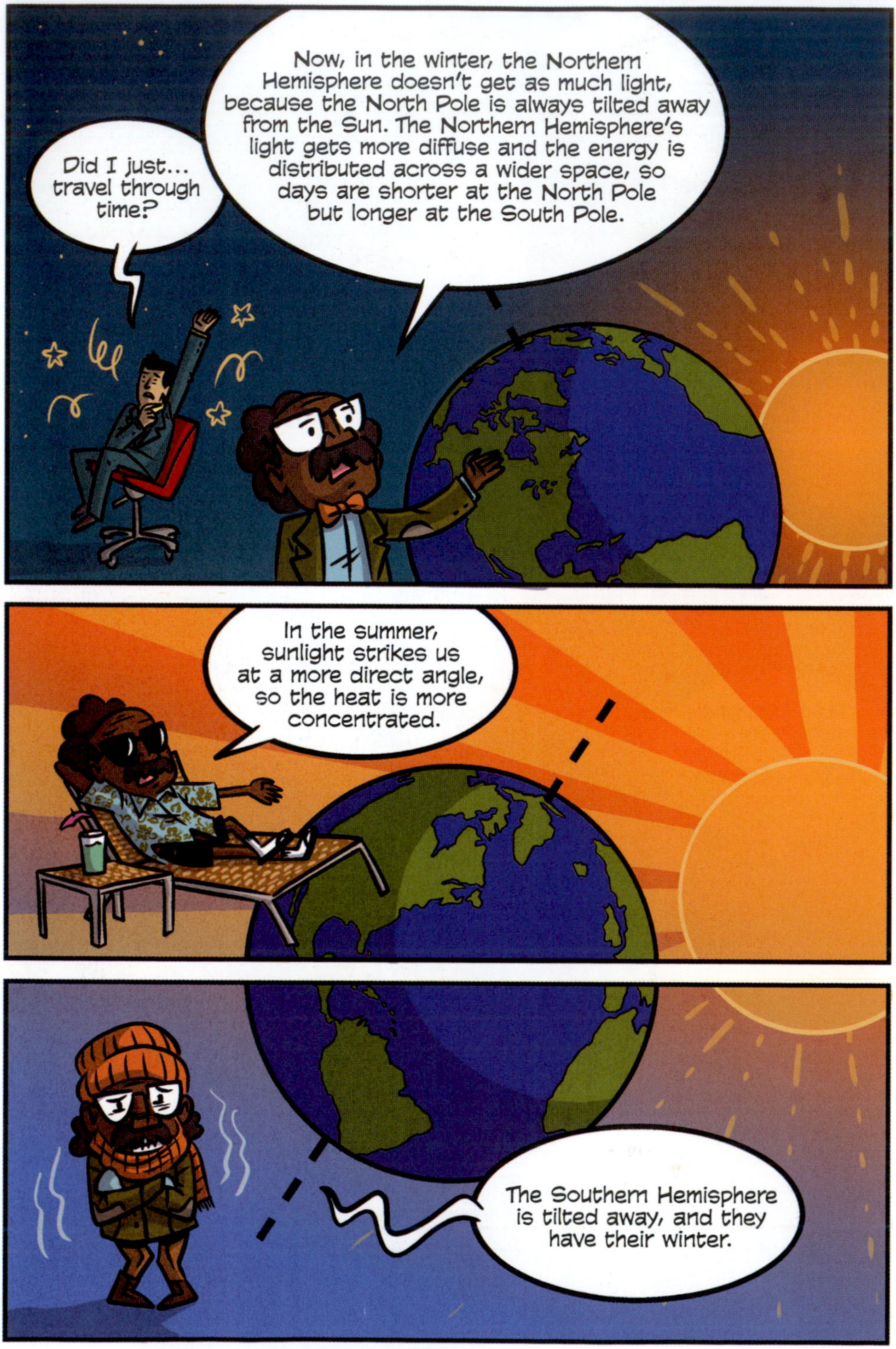
Did I just... travel through time?
Now, in the winter, the Northern Hemisphere doesn't get as much light, because the North Pole is always tilted away from the Sun. The Northern Hemisphere's light gets more diffuse and the energy is distributed across a wider space, so days are shorter at the North Pole but longer at the South Pole.
In the summer, sunlight strikes us at a more direct angle, so the heat is more concentrated.
The Southern Hemisphere is tilted away, and they have their winter.

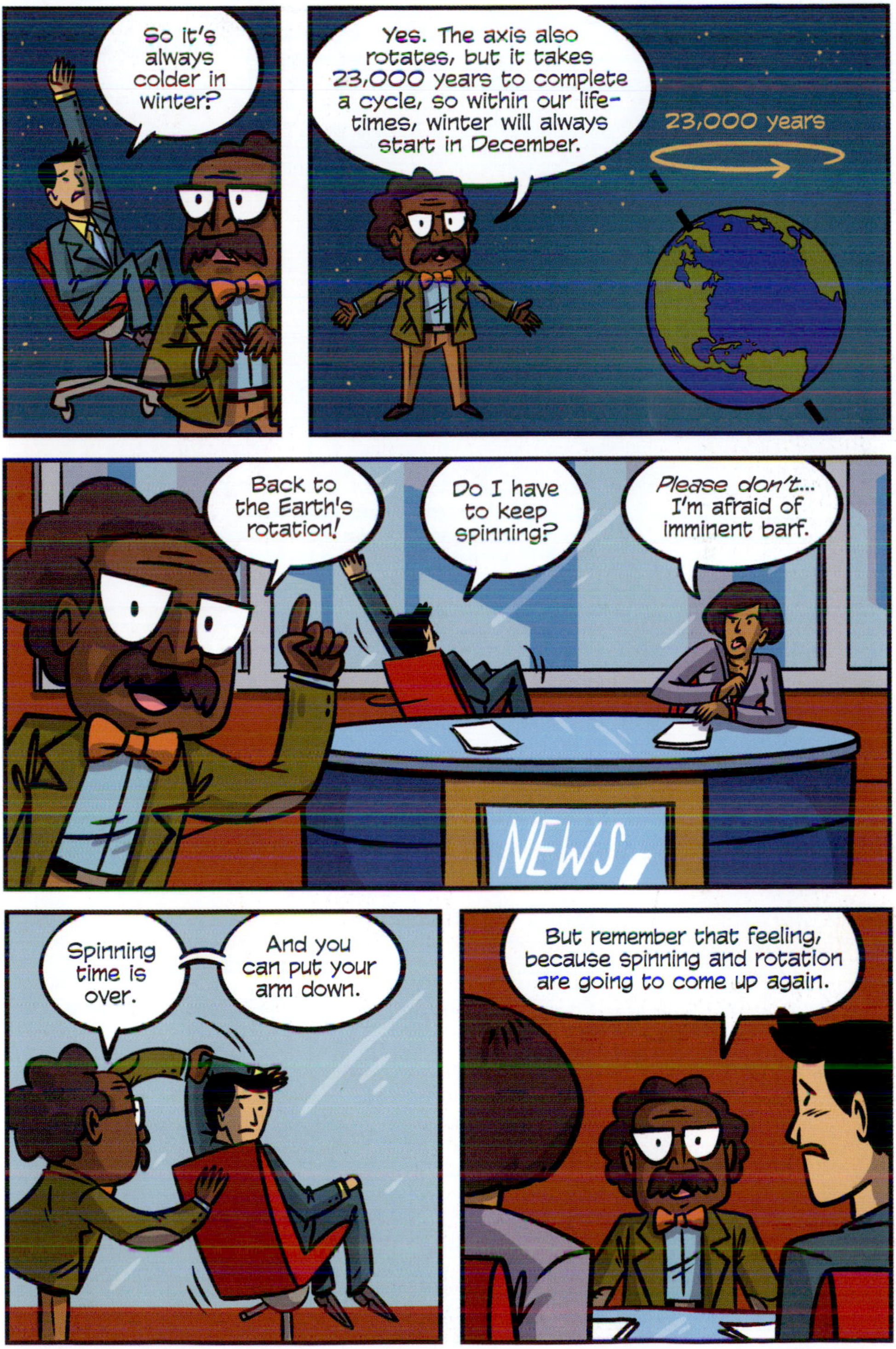
So it's always colder in winter?
Yes. The axis also rotates, but it takes 23,000 years to complete a cycle, so within our lifetimes, winter will always start in December.
23,000 years
Back to the Earth's rotation!
Do I have to keep spinning?
Please don't... I'm afraid of imminent barf.
NEWS
Spinning time is over.
And you can put your arm down.
But remember that feeling, because spinning and rotation are going to come up again.

First we need to know about *heat*.

And how do we measure how hot it is?

Thermometers!

But what do thermometers measure?

...

Say temperature!

TEMPERATURE!

Yes! In the USA, we usually use the Fahrenheit scale, but Celsius is more commonly used in other countries and in science because it's easier to talk about the freezing point of water.

What's the freezing point of water?

32° Fahrenheit, 0° Celsius!

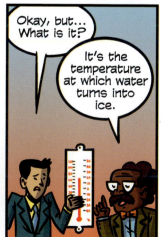

Okay, but... What is it?

It's the temperature at which water turns into ice.

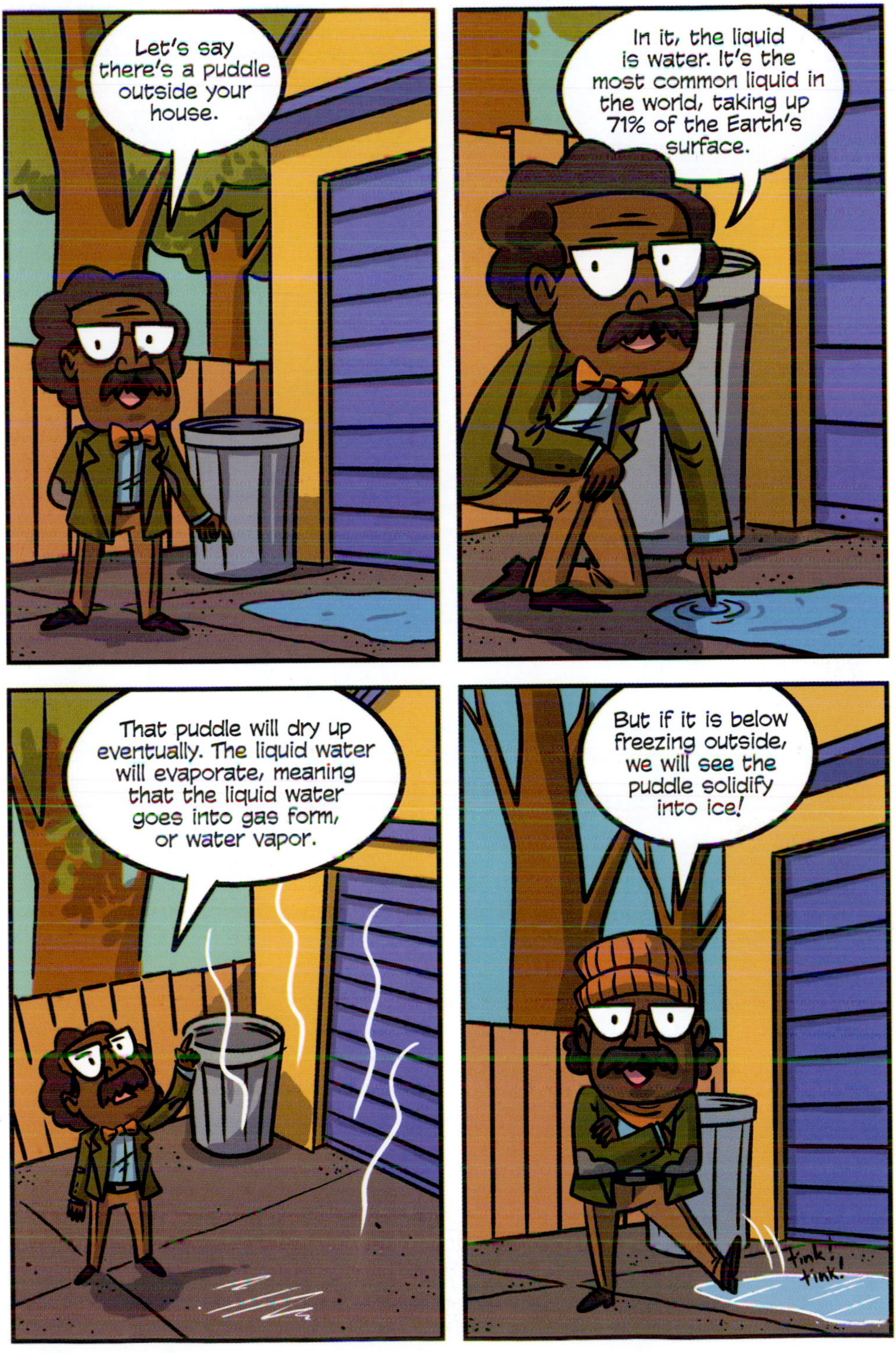
Let's say there's a puddle outside your house.
In it, the liquid is water. It's the most common liquid in the world, taking up 71% of the Earth's surface.
That puddle will dry up eventually. The liquid water will evaporate, meaning that the liquid water goes into gas form, or water vapor.
But if it is below freezing outside, we will see the puddle solidify into ice!
tink! tink!

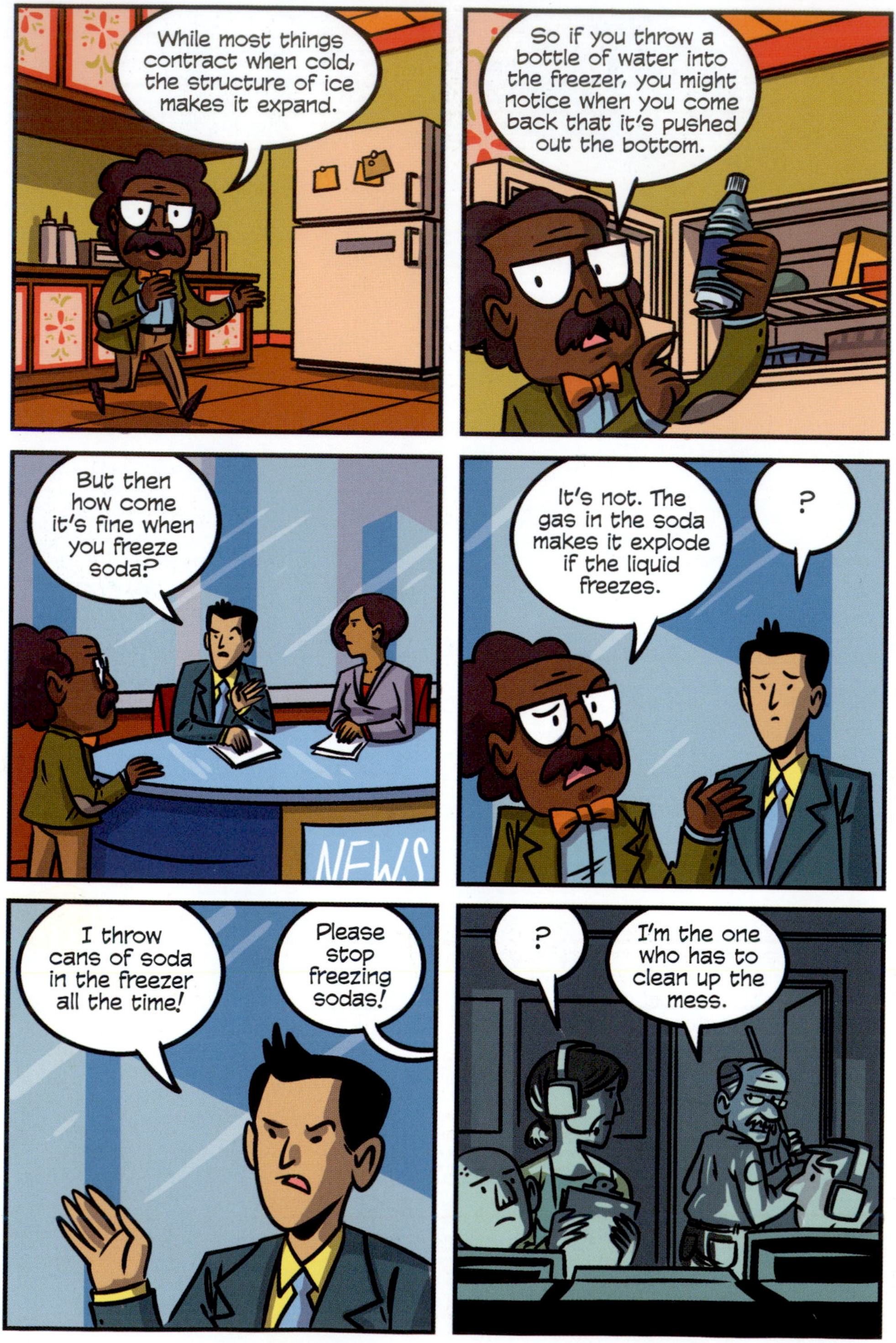
While most things contract when cold, the structure of ice makes it expand.
So if you throw a bottle of water into the freezer, you might notice when you come back that it's pushed out the bottom.
But then how come it's fine when you freeze soda?
NEWS
It's not. The gas in the soda makes it explode if the liquid freezes.
?
I throw cans of soda in the freezer all the time!
Please stop freezing sodas!
?
I'm the one who has to clean up the mess.

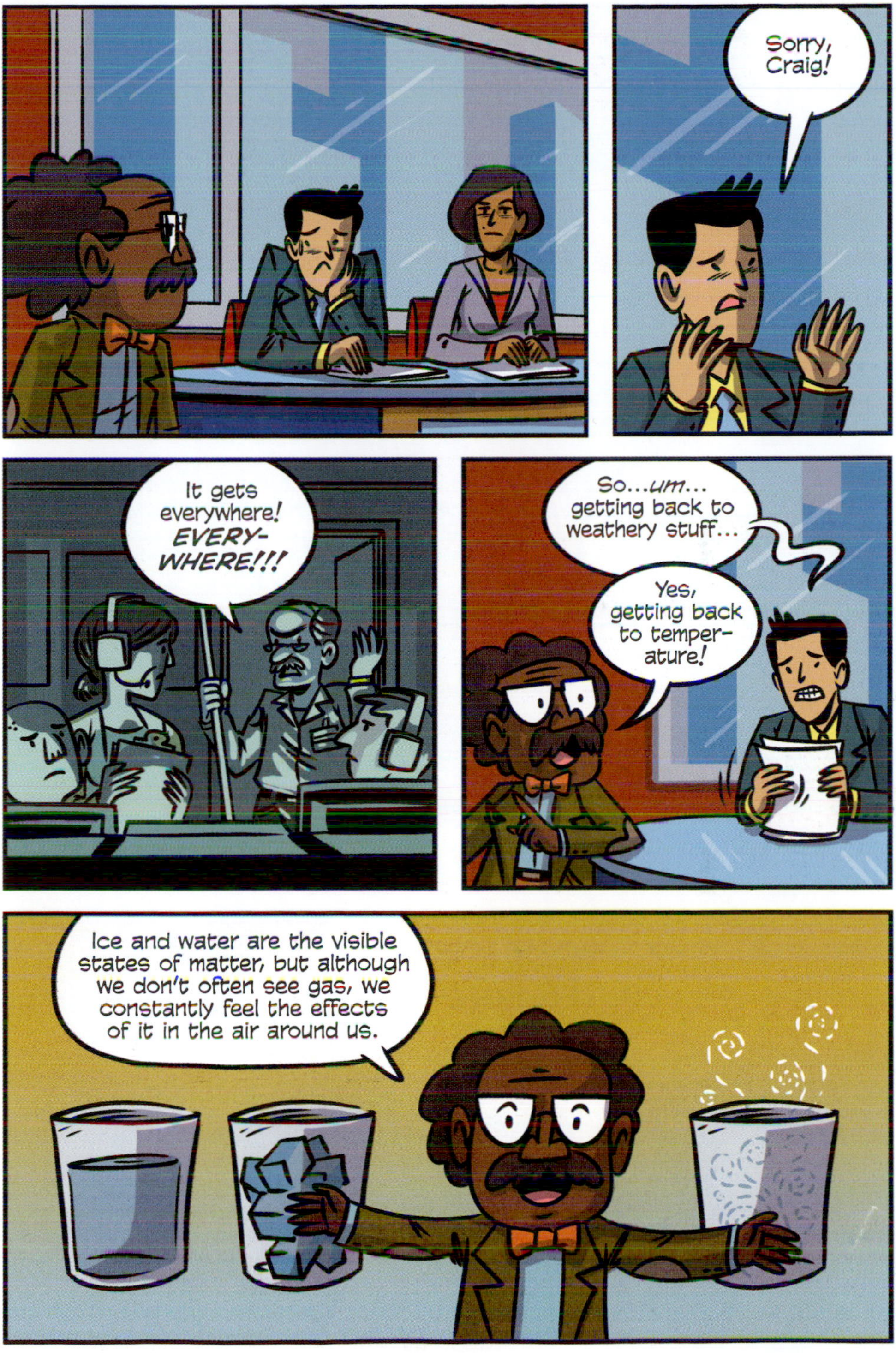

Sorry, Craig!
It gets everywhere! EVERY-WHERE!!!
So...um... getting back to weathery stuff...
Yes, getting back to temper-ature!
Ice and water are the visible states of matter, but although we don't often see gas, we constantly feel the effects of it in the air around us.

Air molecules respond to temperature sort of the same way we do.
In *cold temperatures,* molecules slow down and get closer to each other.
S-s-s-so c-c-c- cold-d-d
Hold me!
In *hot weather,* they speed up and move apart.
Too hot! Don't touch me!
You're too close!

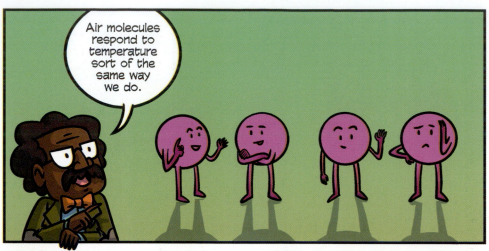

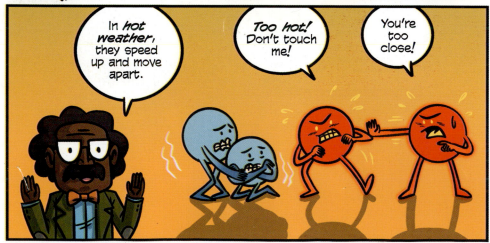

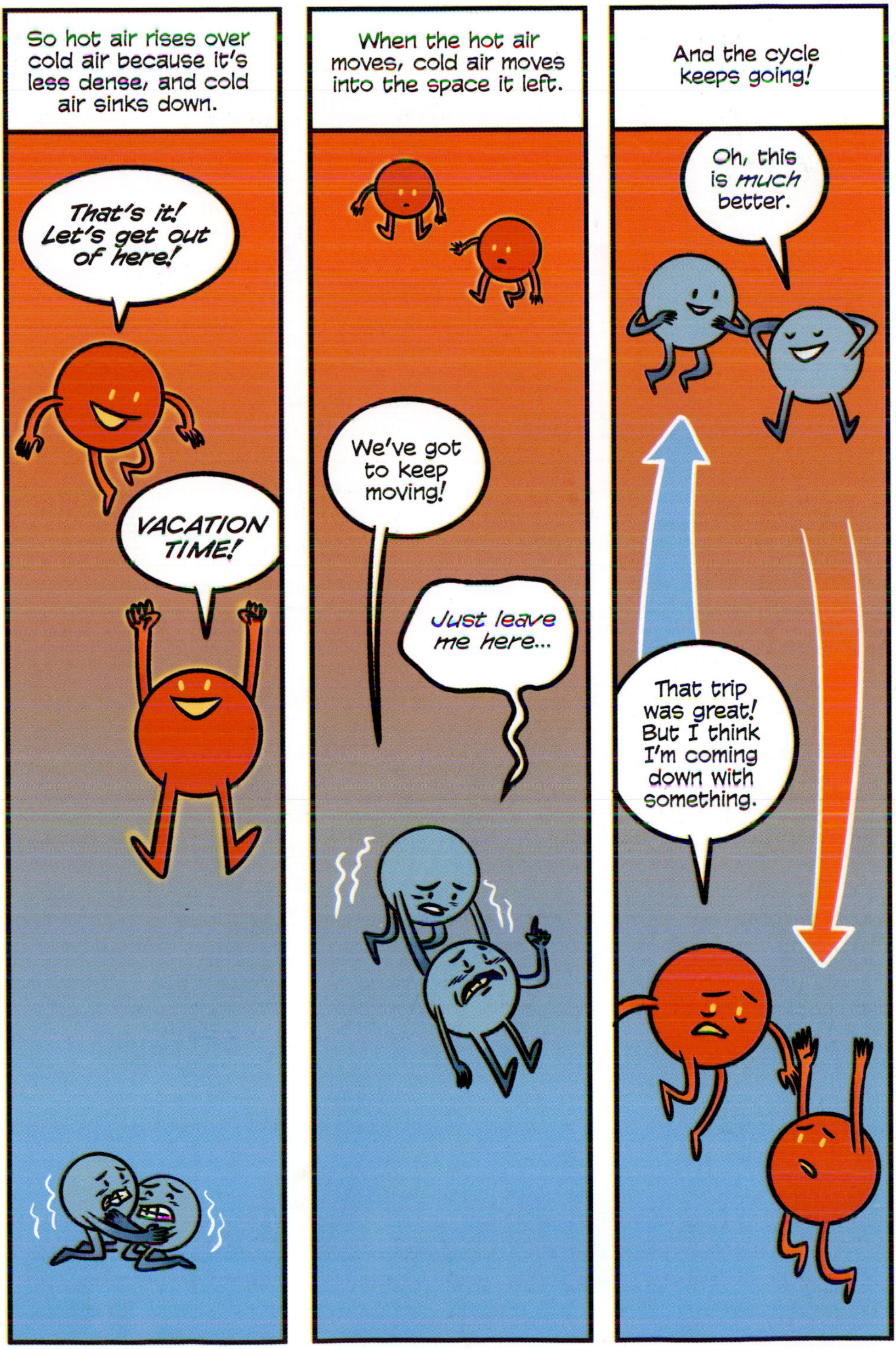
So hot air rises over cold air because it's less dense, and cold air sinks down.
That's it! Let's get out of here!
VACATION TIME!
When the hot air moves, cold air moves into the space it left.
We've got to keep moving!
Just leave me here...
And the cycle keeps going!
Oh, this is *much* better.
That trip was great! But I think I'm coming down with something.

Is this global warming?

No, it's just regular cooling and warming, but it does happen all over the globe!

And these molecules are getting their heat from the Sun?

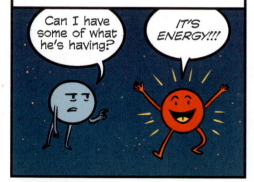

Yes, but on the atomic level, heat is really energy that causes the electrons to move faster.

Can I have some of what he's having?

IT'S ENERGY!!!

Sunlight is delivering this energy, and then depending on where it hits the Earth, the amount of energy striking an area will—

...

Sorry. Too technical?

Yes.

Okay, here's the important concept to take away: different landscapes affect how much heat is absorbed.

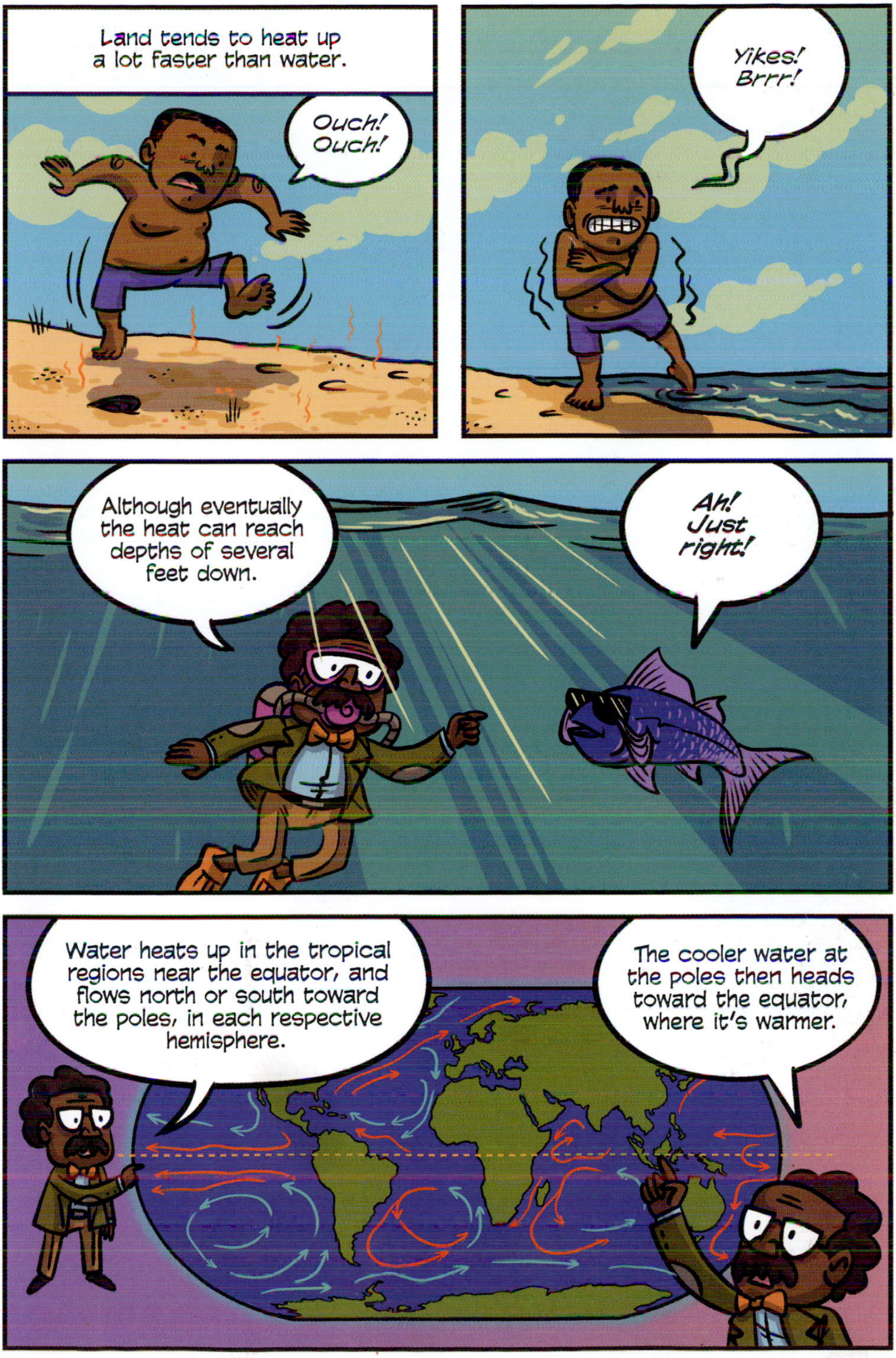
Land tends to heat up a lot faster than water.
Ouch! Ouch!
Yikes! Brrr!
Although eventually the heat can reach depths of several feet down.
Ah! Just right!
Water heats up in the tropical regions near the equator, and flows north or south toward the poles, in each respective hemisphere.
The cooler water at the poles then heads toward the equator, where it's warmer.

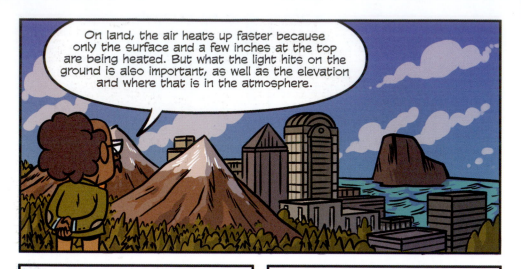

On land, the air heats up faster because only the surface and a few inches at the top are being heated. But what the light hits on the ground is also important, as well as the elevation and where that is in the atmosphere.

It's colder at the top of mountains than it is at sea level because you're higher in the atmosphere.

Mountains also create physical barriers, causing wind to be funneled through passes.

Snow and anything with a white surface keep the ground from absorbing more heat by reflecting light back up.

Man-made structures like buildings and roads—especially heat-absorbing black asphalt—change how heat is absorbed on the ground.

Ouch! Ouch!

Maybe you should start wearing shoes.

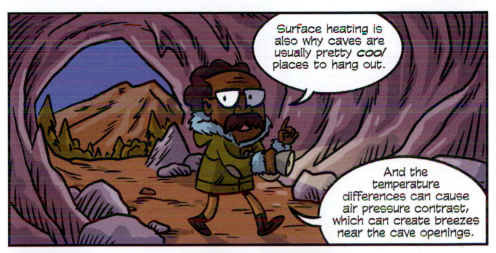

Surface heating is also why caves are usually pretty *cool* places to hang out.

And the temperature differences can cause air pressure contrast, which can create breezes near the cave openings.

Back up a second. What's *air pressure?*

Air pressure is the weight of all the air on us being pulled down by gravity.

We don't often think about it because it's invisible, but it's a force being exerted on you all the time.

Like fame...

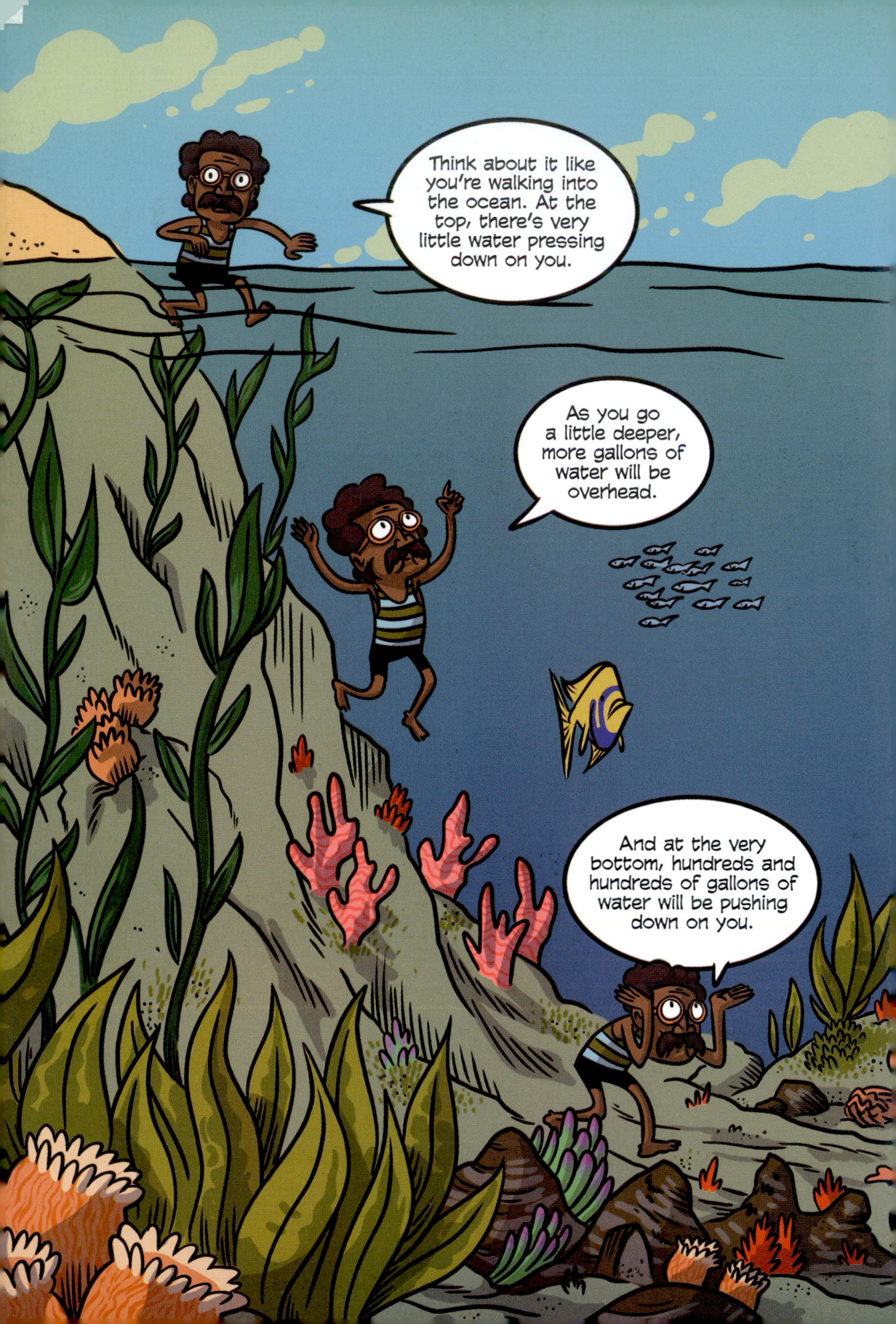
Think about it like you're walking into the ocean. At the top, there's very little water pressing down on you.
As you go a little deeper, more gallons of water will be overhead.
And at the very bottom, hundreds and hundreds of gallons of water will be pushing down on you.

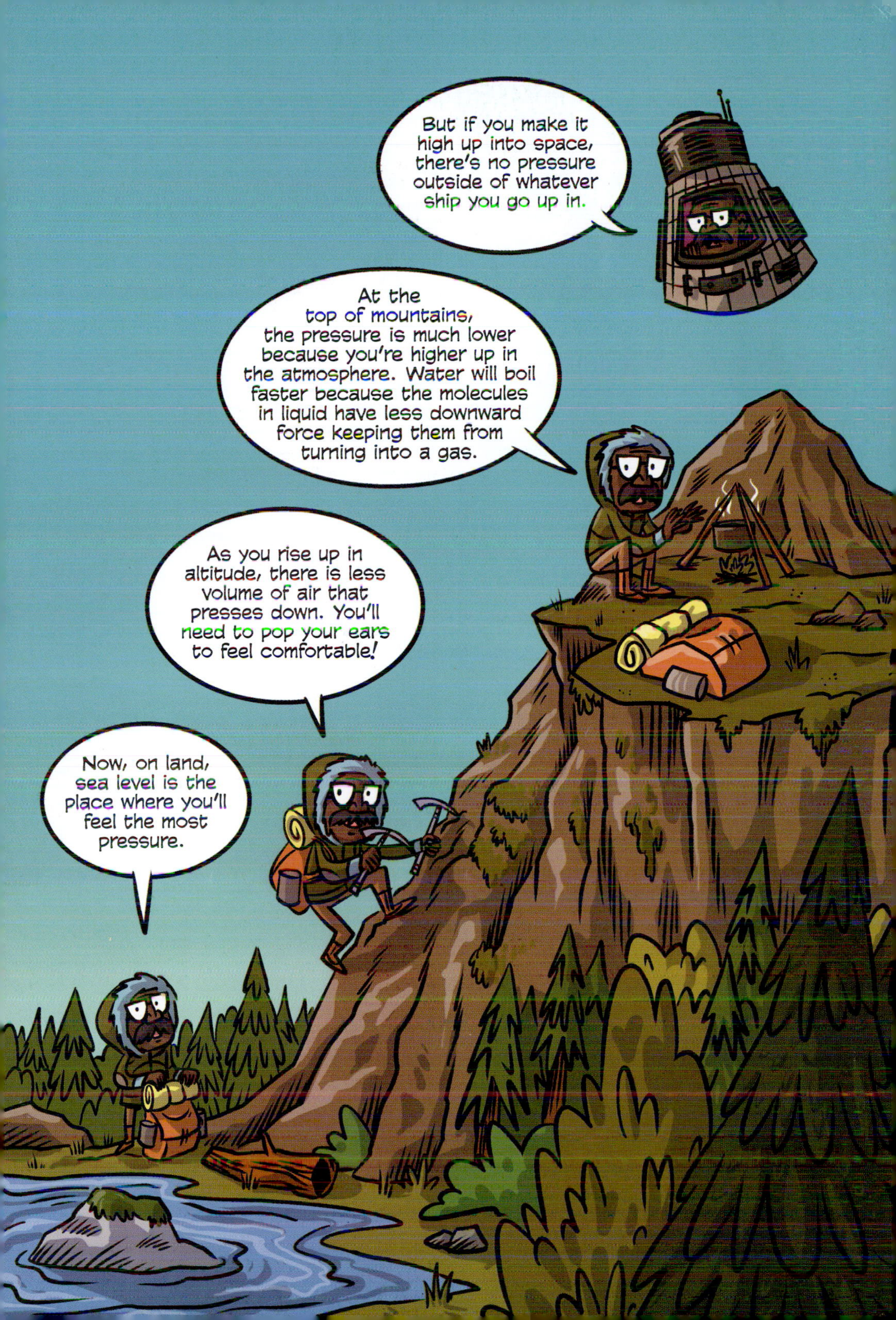

Now, on land, sea level is the place where you'll feel the most pressure.
As you rise up in altitude, there is less volume of air that presses down. You'll need to pop your ears to feel comfortable!
At the top of mountains, the pressure is much lower because you're higher up in the atmosphere. Water will boil faster because the molecules in liquid have less downward force keeping them from turning into a gas.
But if you make it high up into space, there's no pressure outside of whatever ship you go up in.

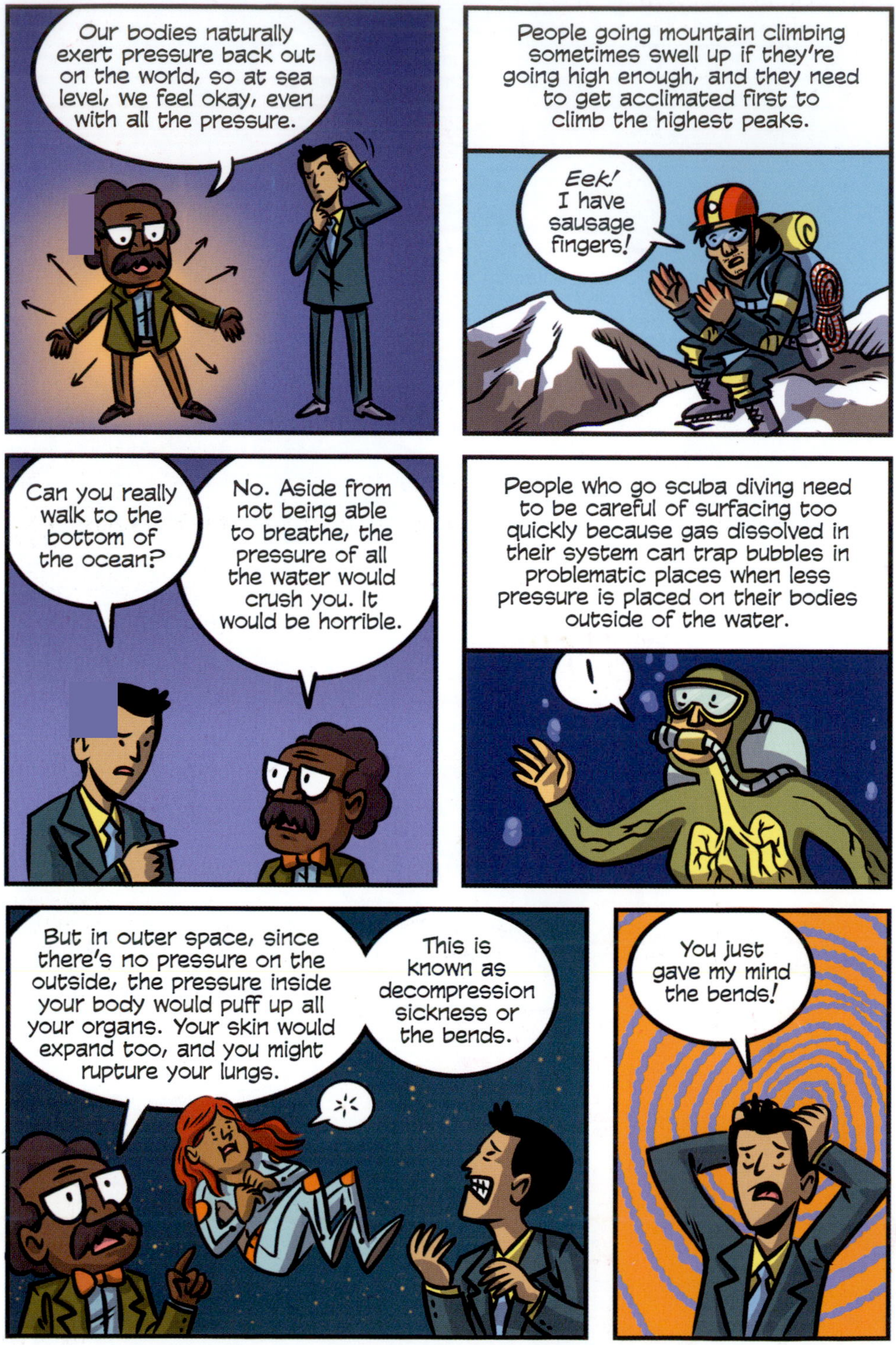
Our bodies naturally exert pressure back out on the world, so at sea level, we feel okay, even with all the pressure.
People going mountain climbing sometimes swell up if they're going high enough, and they need to get acclimated first to climb the highest peaks.
Eek! I have sausage fingers!
Can you really walk to the bottom of the ocean?
No. Aside from not being able to breathe, the pressure of all the water would crush you. It would be horrible.
People who go scuba diving need to be careful of surfacing too quickly because gas dissolved in their system can trap bubbles in problematic places when less pressure is placed on their bodies outside of the water.
!
But in outer space, since there's no pressure on the outside, the pressure inside your body would puff up all your organs. Your skin would expand too, and you might rupture your lungs.
This is known as decompression sickness or the bends.
You just gave my mind the bends!

Now that you understand what air pressure is, let's talk about how air moves around.

It starts with masses of air with different temperatures.

RUMBLE IN THE ATMOSPHERE ABOVE THE JUNGLE

H VS L

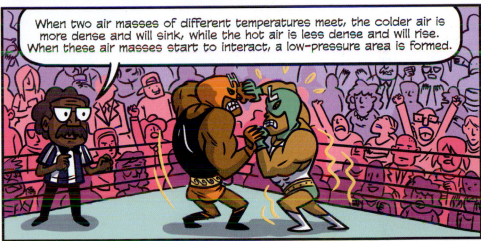

When two air masses of different temperatures meet, the colder air is more dense and will sink, while the hot air is less dense and will rise. When these air masses start to interact, a low-pressure area is formed.

Behind this clash of air masses and stormy low pressure, a high-pressure system with calm conditions often follows.

There doesn't need to be a large difference between the two temperatures either— a couple of degrees is enough to create some movement.

Air moves from the places with high pressure toward areas where there is low pressure. The movement between spots with high and low pressure creates wind!

Really? It's not the rotation of the Earth?

No, but we'll come back to that in a minute. I'm glad you haven't forgotten about it.

When we're speaking about global regions for weather purposes, we break them up by latitudes, which go around the Earth like belts.

Each half of the globe is divided into 90-degree segments.

The equator is set at 0°, and the poles are 90°.

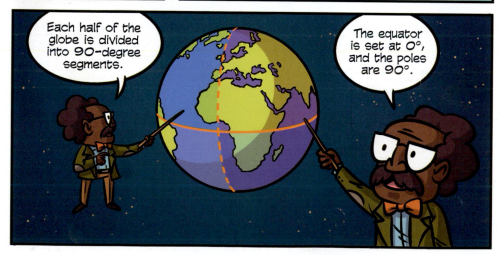

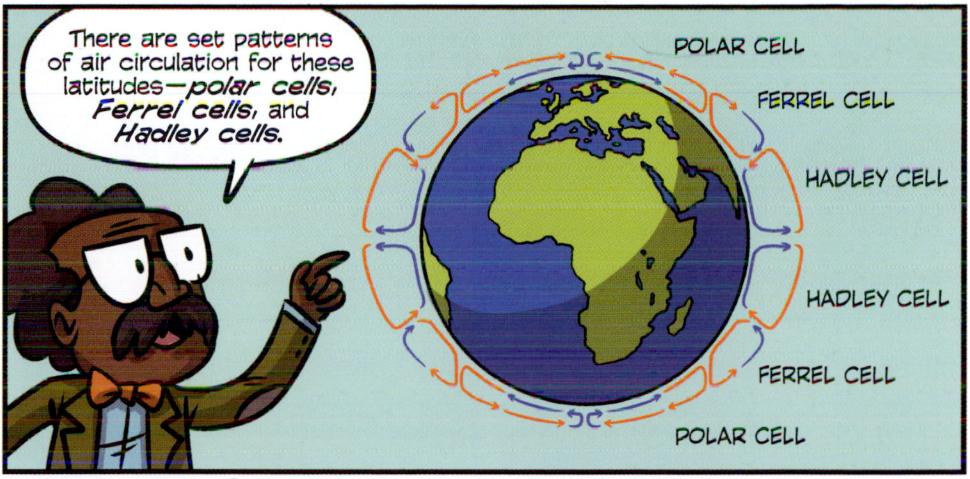
There are set patterns of air circulation for these latitudes—*polar cells, Ferrel cells,* and *Hadley cells.*
POLAR CELL
FERREL CELL
HADLEY CELL
HADLEY CELL
FERREL CELL
POLAR CELL

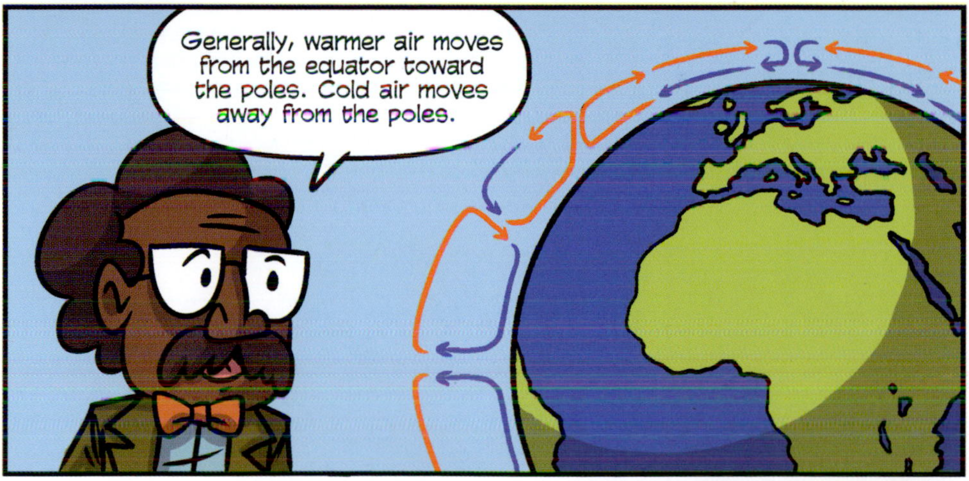
Generally, warmer air moves from the equator toward the poles. Cold air moves away from the poles.

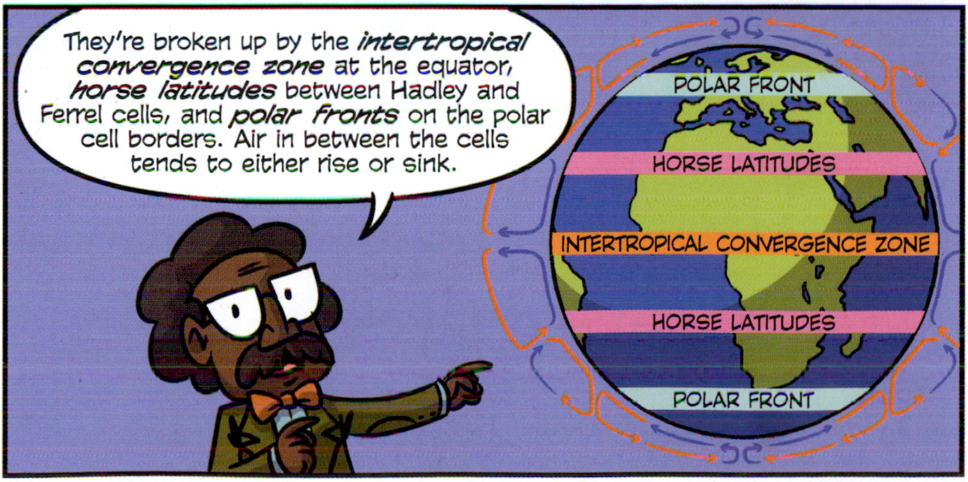
They're broken up by the *intertropical convergence zone* at the equator, *horse latitudes* between Hadley and Ferrel cells, and *polar fronts* on the polar cell borders. Air in between the cells tends to either rise or sink.
POLAR FRONT
HORSE LATITUDES
INTERTROPICAL CONVERGENCE ZONE
HORSE LATITUDES
POLAR FRONT

Getting back to the Earth's roation... We need to talk about the Coriolis effect for a minute.

Since the technical explanation gets into physics, which you're clearly not ready for...

NO! NO, I'M NOT!!!

Let's talk about the effect itself.

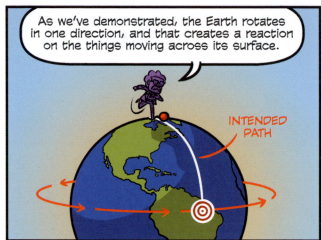

As we've demonstrated, the Earth rotates in one direction, and that creates a reaction on the things moving across its surface.

INTENDED PATH

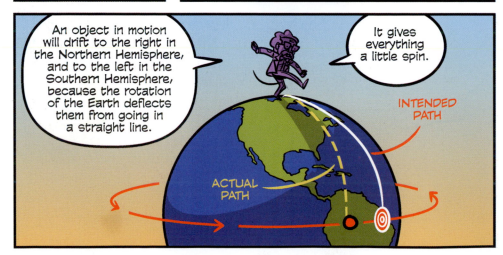

An object in motion will drift to the right in the Northern Hemisphere, and to the left in the Southern Hemisphere, because the rotation of the Earth deflects them from going in a straight line.

It gives everything a little spin.

INTENDED PATH

ACTUAL PATH

Is the Coriolis effect the thing that happens in the toilet when you flush?
Kind of.
The spin of water in your toilet is based on the shape and layout of its parts. Most drains are typically too small to show the effect.
But the Coriolis effect produces a constant, predictable force on the weather. If you're heading north from the equator, you'll veer east, and heading south from the North Pole, you'll veer west.
EQUATOR
Going south from the equator will send you east, and north from the South Pole will send you west.
EQUATOR
It affects masses of air all the time, and there are even a set of names for the wind that correlates to the convection cells.
EASTERLIES
WESTERLIES
NE TRADE WINDS
SE TRADE WINDS
WESTERLIES
EASTERLIES

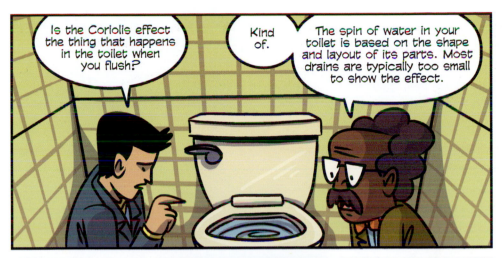

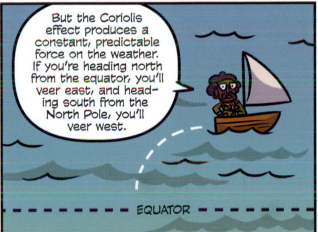

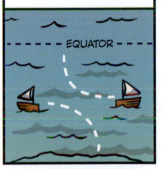

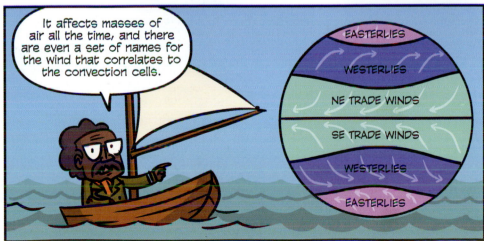

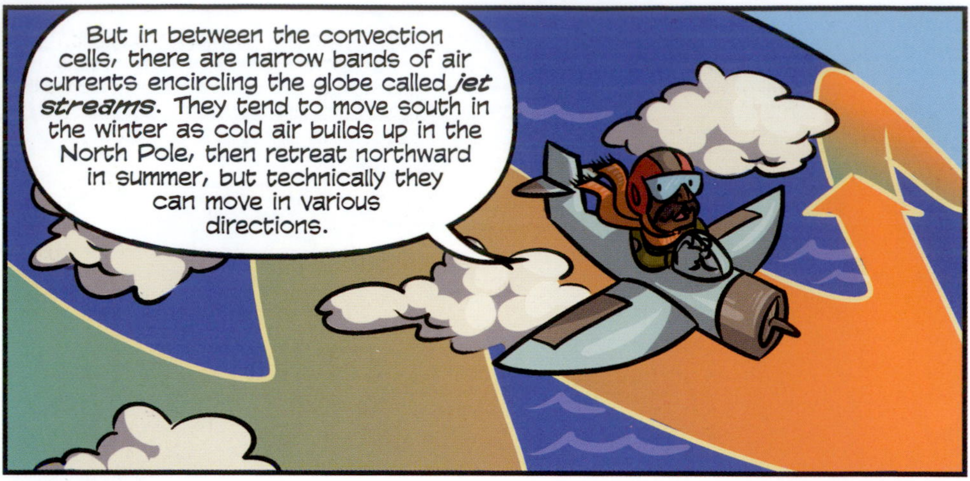
But in between the convection cells, there are narrow bands of air currents encircling the globe called *jet streams*. They tend to move south in the winter as cold air builds up in the North Pole, then retreat northward in summer, but technically they can move in various directions.

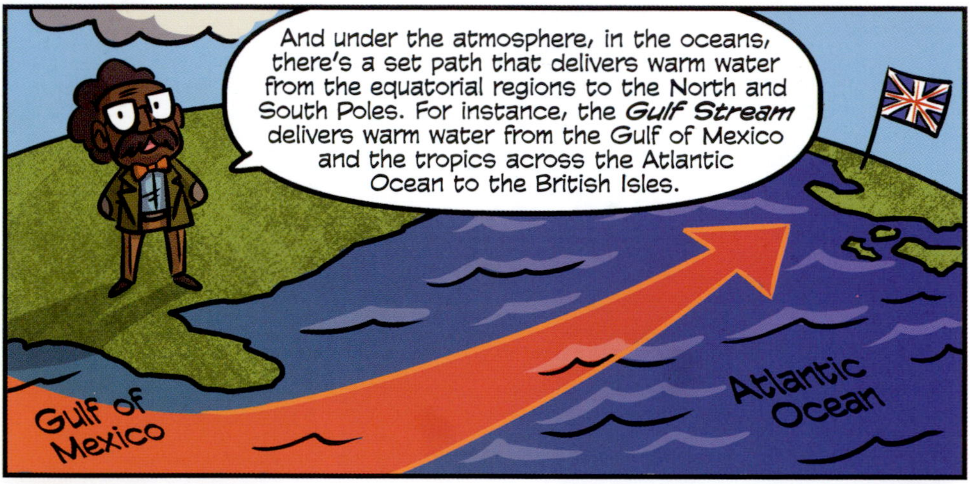
And under the atmosphere, in the oceans, there's a set path that delivers warm water from the equatorial regions to the North and South Poles. For instance, the *Gulf Stream* delivers warm water from the Gulf of Mexico and the tropics across the Atlantic Ocean to the British Isles.
Gulf of Mexico
Atlantic Ocean

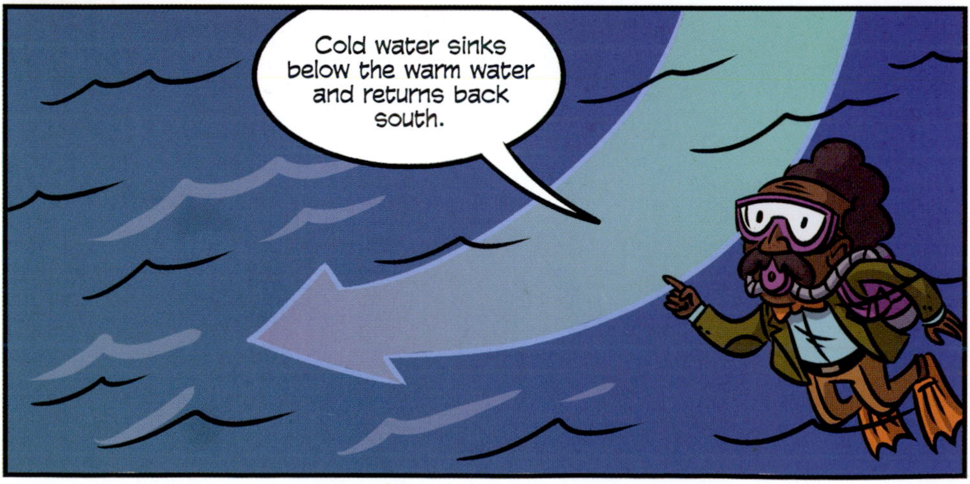
Cold water sinks below the warm water and returns back south.

Norman, what does *any* of this have to do with global warming?!

Well, I'm getting there...

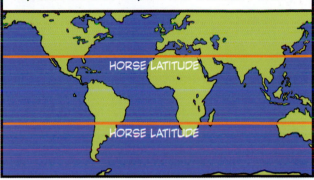

...but one thing about the horse latitudes is that their location correspond to most of the major deserts in the world, including the Sahara, Kalahari, Syrian, Atacama, Mojave, and Sonoran Deserts.

HORSE LATITUDE

HORSE LATITUDE

So those places are locked into patterns where they receive a lot of sun and dry weather.

Deserts are hot. Got it.

I'm sorry... am I *boring you*?!

We're *ACTION* news! When do we get to the action?

Fine.

Let's talk about fronts. There are *warm fronts* and *cold fronts.*

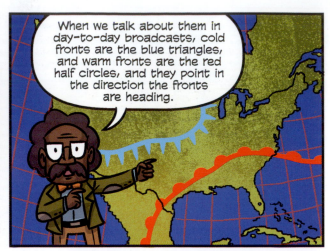

When we talk about them in day-to-day broadcasts, cold fronts are the blue triangles, and warm fronts are the red half circles, and they point in the direction the fronts are heading.

Cold and warm air don't mix together when they meet. Warm air slides on top of the cold air in a gentle slope at a warm front.

WARM AIR

COLD AIR

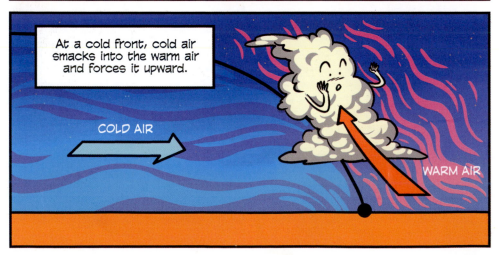

At a cold front, cold air smacks into the warm air and forces it upward.

COLD AIR

WARM AIR

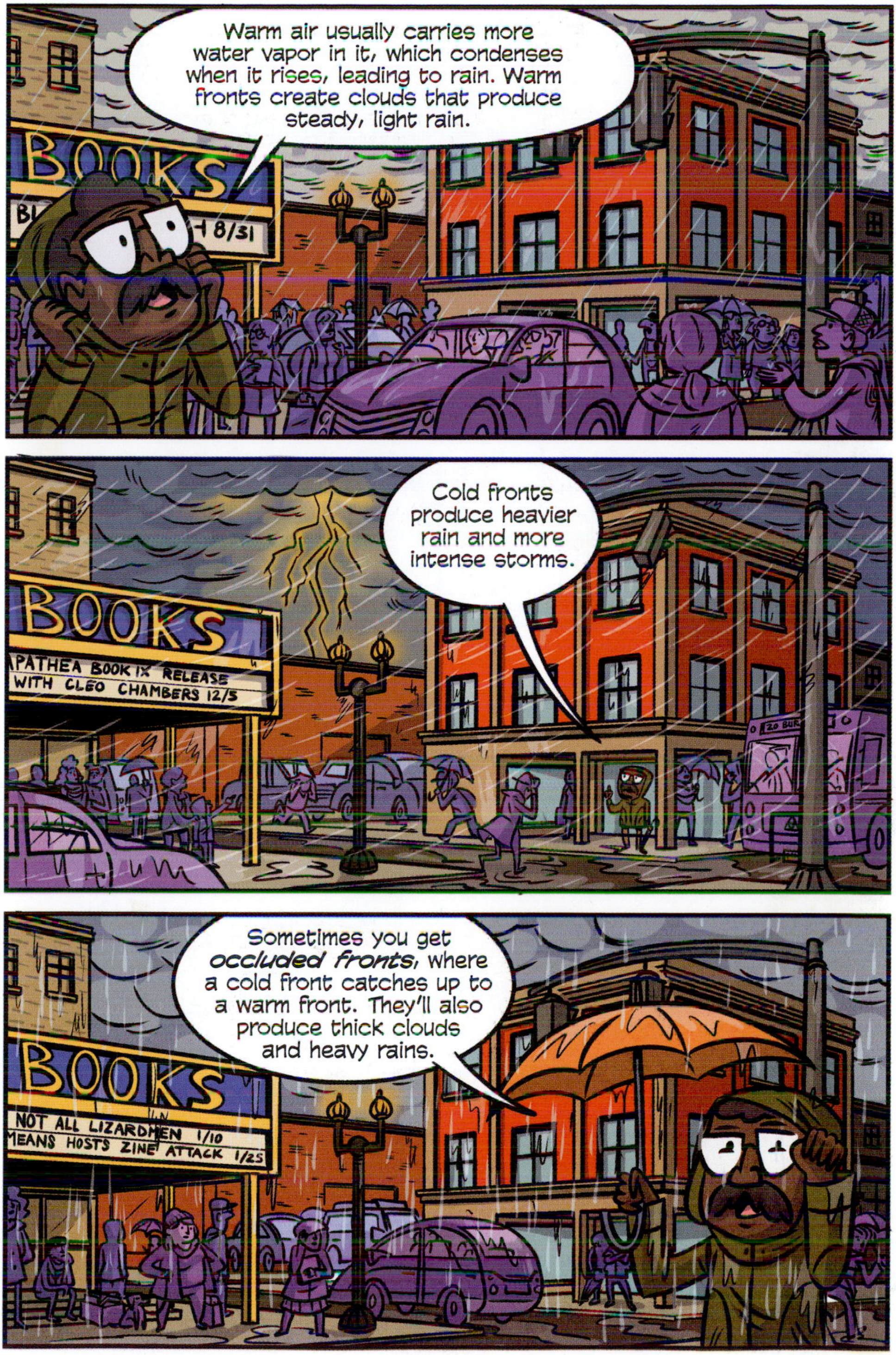
Warm air usually carries more water vapor in it, which condenses when it rises, leading to rain. Warm fronts create clouds that produce steady, light rain.
BOOKS
Cold fronts produce heavier rain and more intense storms.
BOOKS
PATHEA BOOK IX RELEASE
WITH CLEO CHAMBERS 12/5
Sometimes you get *occluded fronts*, where a cold front catches up to a warm front. They'll also produce thick clouds and heavy rains.
BOOKS
NOT ALL LIZARDMEN 1/10
MEANS HOSTS ZINE ATTACK 1/25

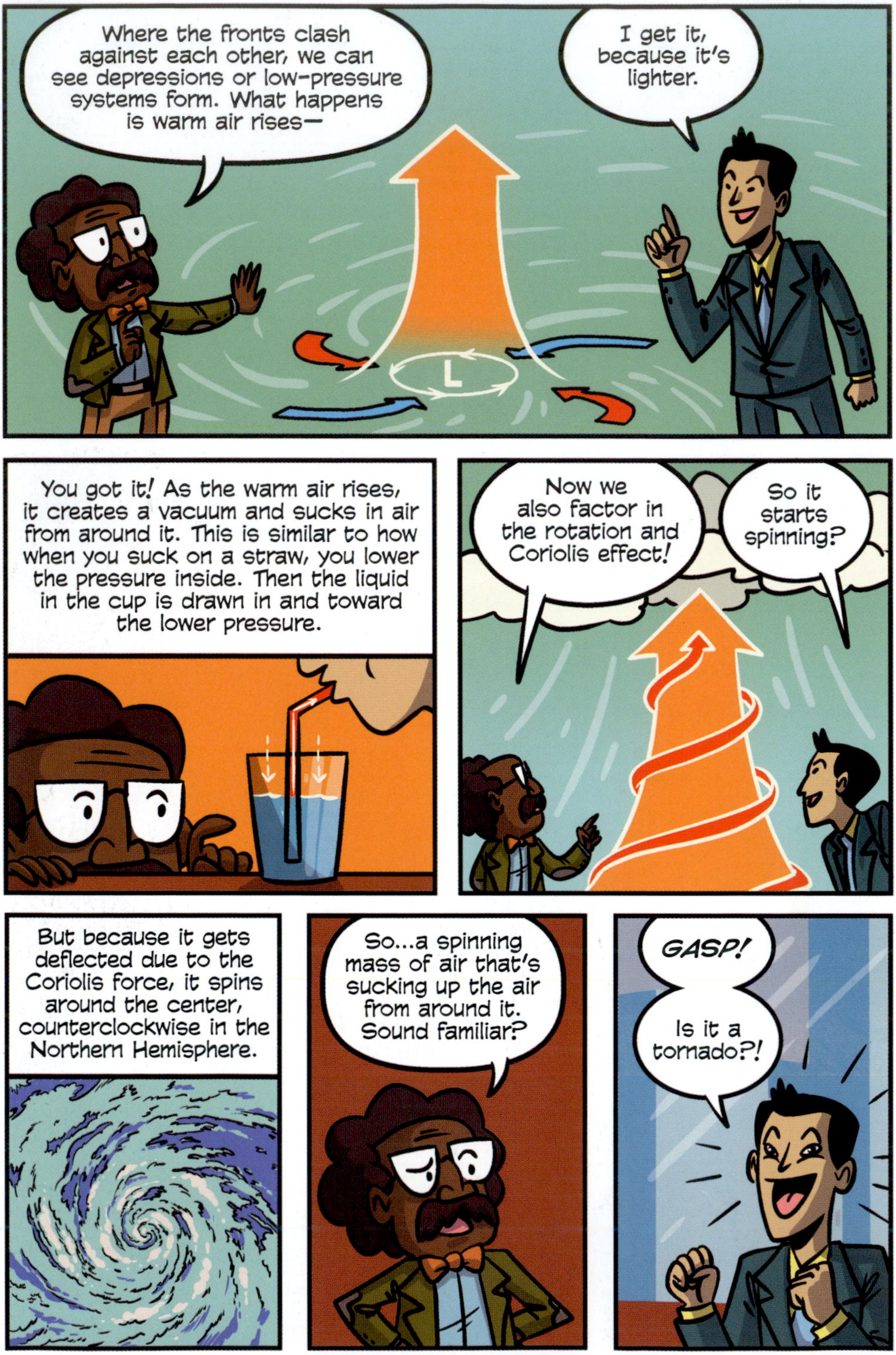
Where the fronts clash against each other, we can see depressions or low-pressure systems form. What happens is warm air rises—
I get it, because it's lighter.
L
You got it! As the warm air rises, it creates a vacuum and sucks in air from around it. This is similar to how when you suck on a straw, you lower the pressure inside. Then the liquid in the cup is drawn in and toward the lower pressure.
Now we also factor in the rotation and Coriolis effect!
So it starts spinning?
But because it gets deflected due to the Coriolis force, it spins around the center, counterclockwise in the Northern Hemisphere.
So...a spinning mass of air that's sucking up the air from around it. Sound familiar?
GASP!
Is it a tornado?!

It is! The opposite of that is the high-pressure zone and the anticyclone forces, which—

BLAH BLAH BLAH

They go down and go the opposite way and they're normal and boring and I don't care. Tell me more about *tornadoes!*

He's right, Norman. Give us a little excitement.

Okay, okay. I was getting there anyway.

Yes! Tell me, are we in danger of a tornado during the *SNOWPOCALYPSE?* How fast are they? Do you think I can outrun one? I ran varsity track in high school!

First, tornadoes are more frequent in the late spring and summer, so we're probably not going to experience one anytime soon.

Hmph!

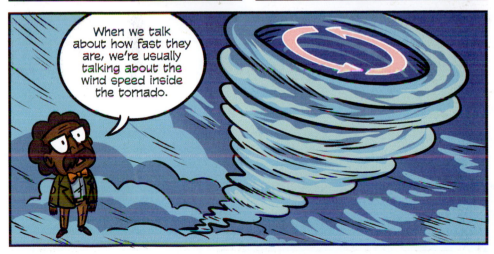

When we talk about how fast they are, we're usually talking about the wind speed inside the tornado.

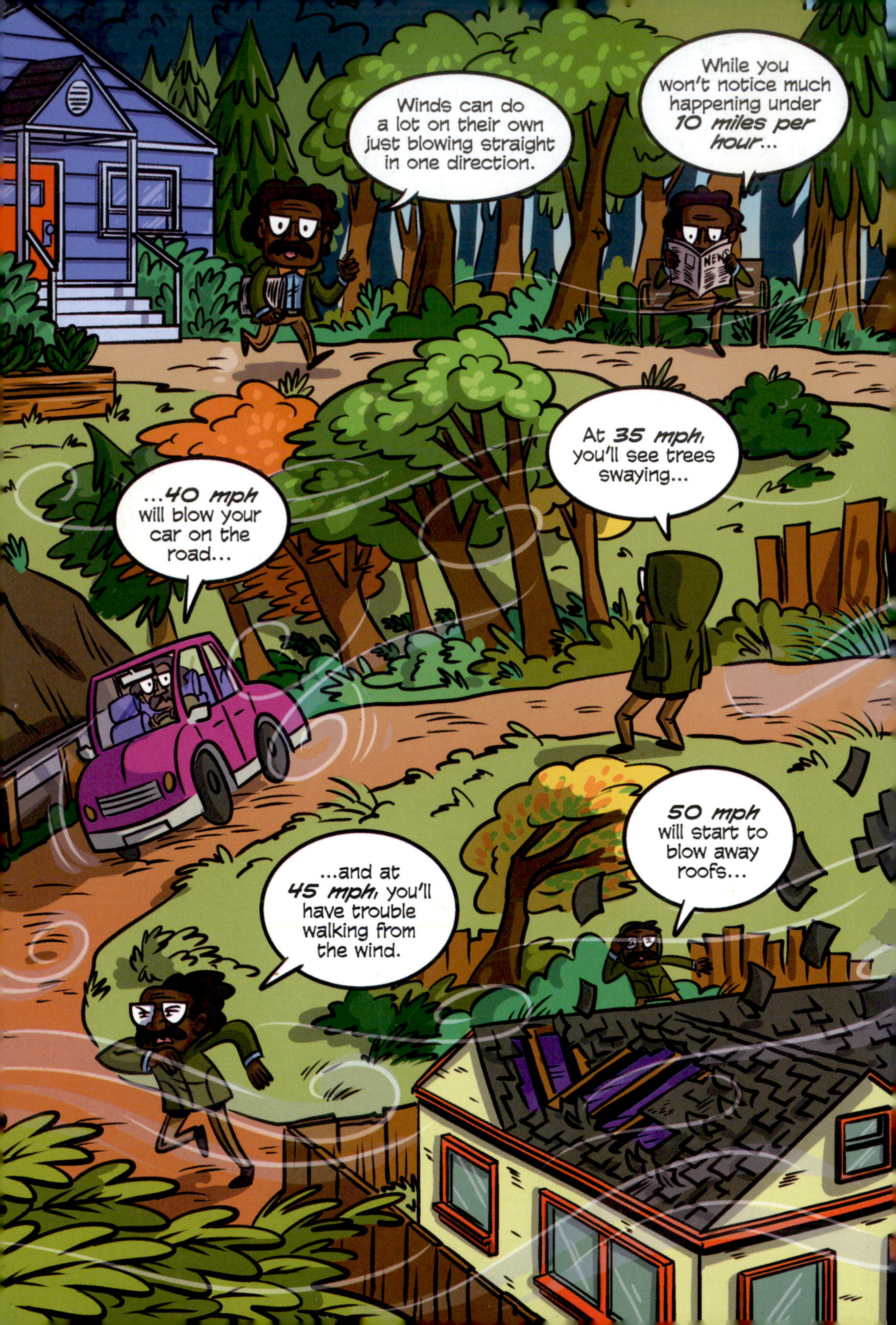
Winds can do a lot on their own just blowing straight in one direction.
While you won't notice much happening under *10 miles per hour*...
NEWS
At *35 mph*, you'll see trees swaying...
...*40 mph* will blow your car on the road...
50 mph will start to blow away roofs...
...and at *45 mph*, you'll have trouble walking from the wind.

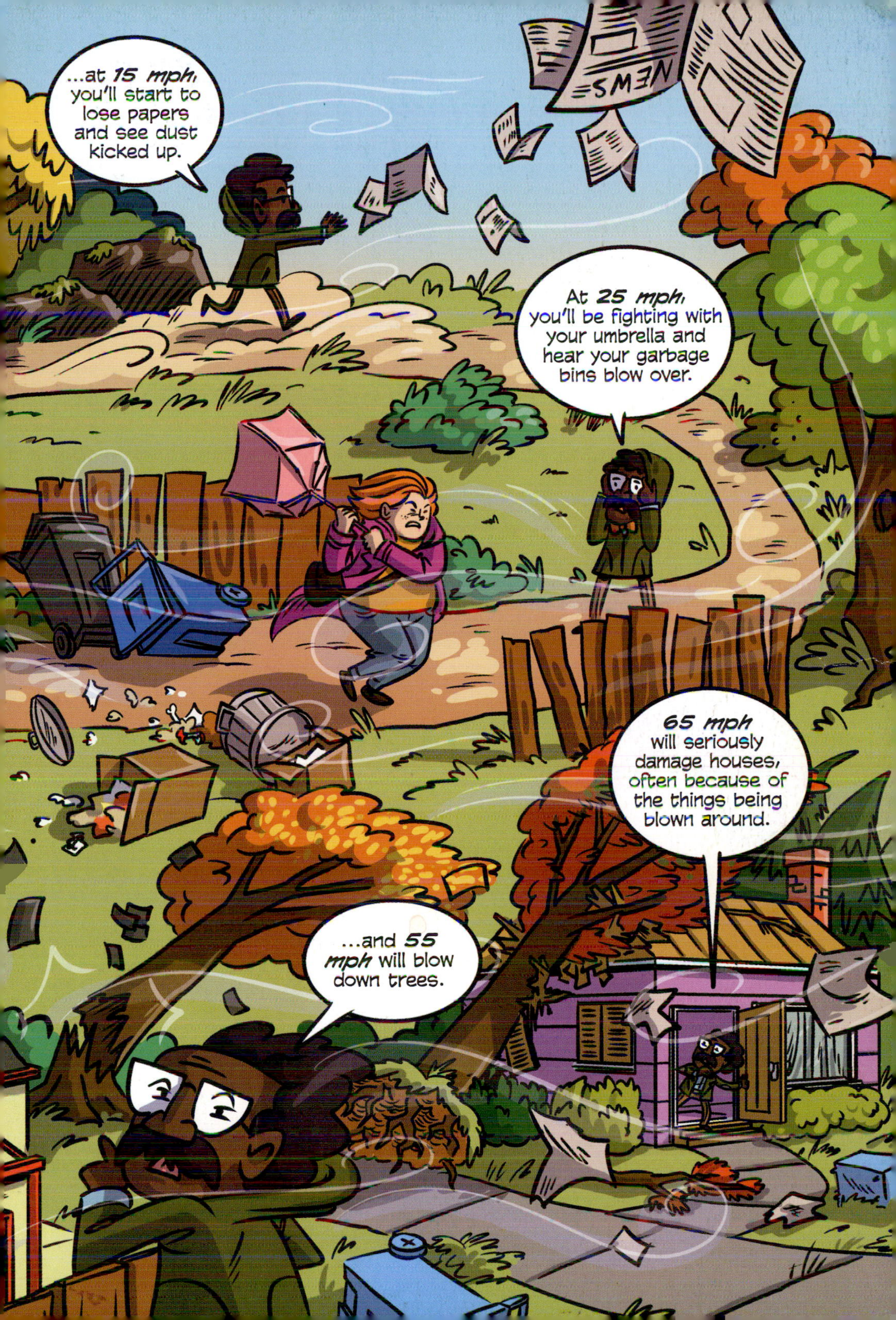

NEWS
...at *15 mph,* you'll start to lose papers and see dust kicked up.
At *25 mph,* you'll be fighting with your umbrella and hear your garbage bins blow over.
...and *55 mph* will blow down trees.
65 mph will seriously damage houses, often because of the things being blown around.

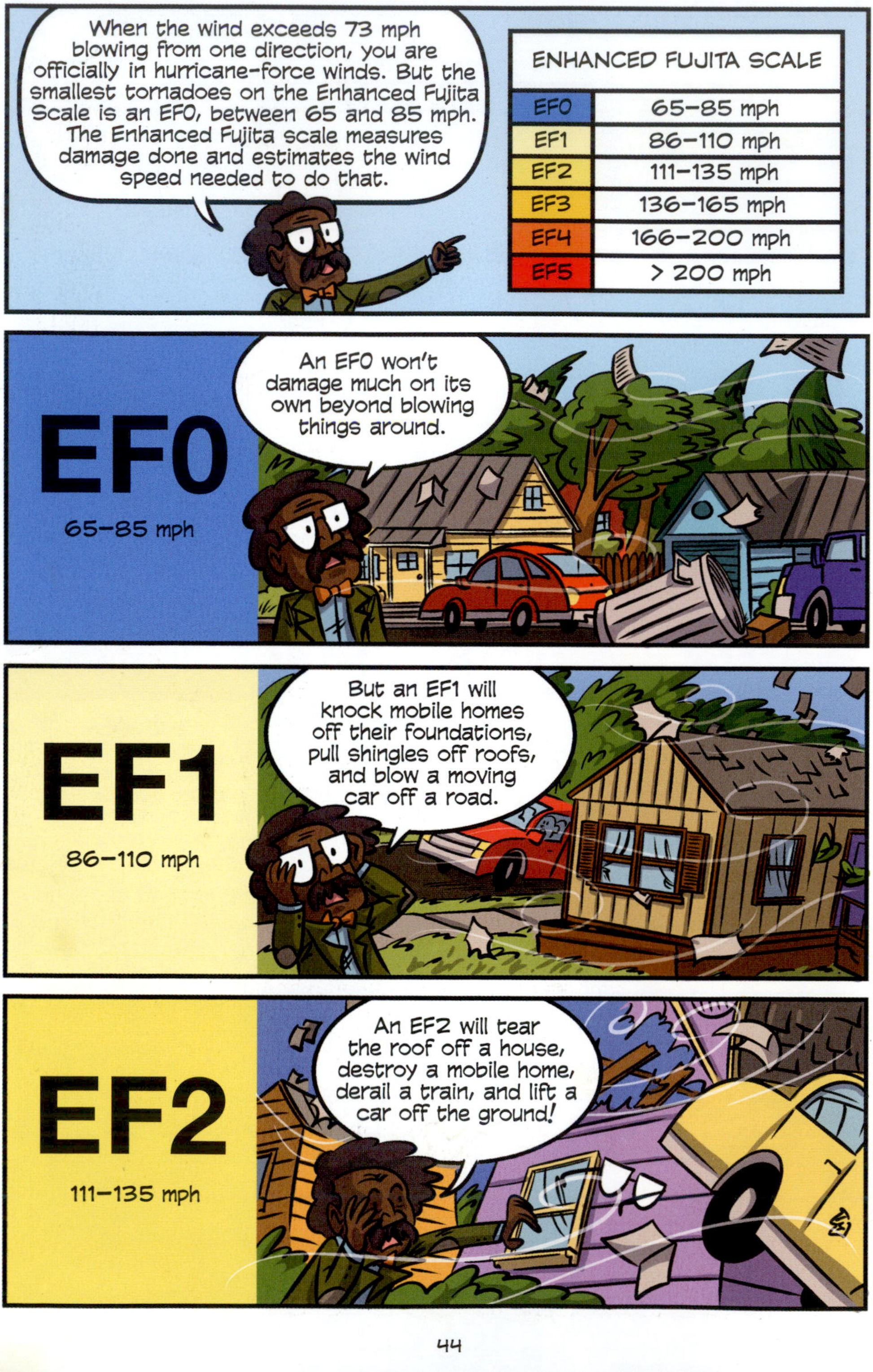
When the wind exceeds 73 mph blowing from one direction, you are officially in hurricane-force winds. But the smallest tornadoes on the Enhanced Fujita Scale is an EF0, between 65 and 85 mph. The Enhanced Fujita scale measures damage done and estimates the wind speed needed to do that.

ENHANCED FUJITA SCALE	
EF0	65–85 mph
EF1	86–110 mph
EF2	111–135 mph
EF3	136–165 mph
EF4	166–200 mph
EF5	> 200 mph

EF0
65–85 mph
An EF0 won't damage much on its own beyond blowing things around.
EF1
86–110 mph
But an EF1 will knock mobile homes off their foundations, pull shingles off roofs, and blow a moving car off a road.
EF2
111–135 mph
An EF2 will tear the roof off a house, destroy a mobile home, derail a train, and lift a car off the ground!

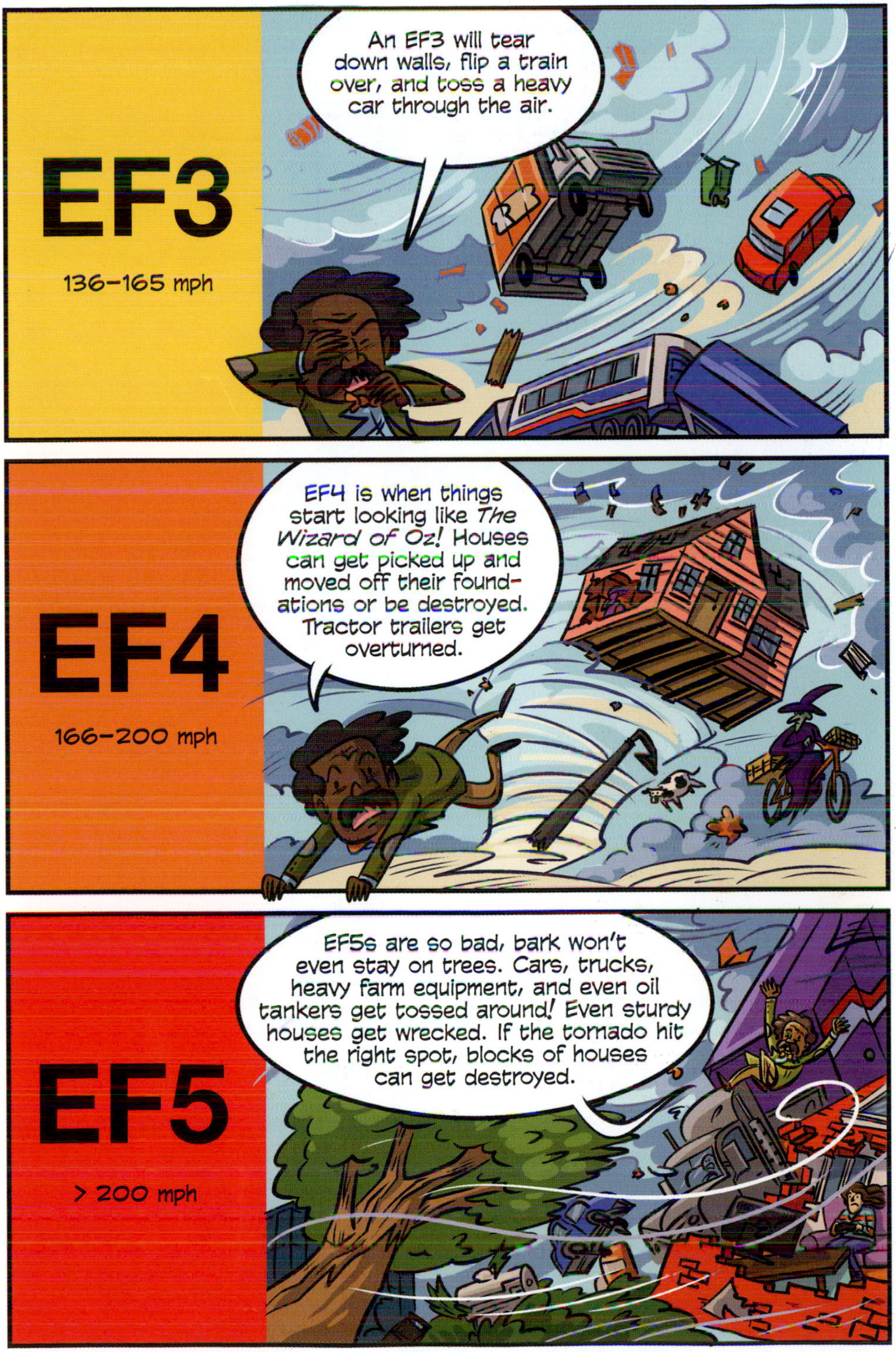
EF3
136–165 mph
An EF3 will tear down walls, flip a train over, and toss a heavy car through the air.
EF4
166–200 mph
EF4 is when things start looking like *The Wizard of Oz!* Houses can get picked up and moved off their foundations or be destroyed. Tractor trailers get overturned.
EF5
> 200 mph
EF5s are so bad, bark won't even stay on trees. Cars, trucks, heavy farm equipment, and even oil tankers get tossed around! Even sturdy houses get wrecked. If the tornado hit the right spot, blocks of houses can get destroyed.

So do you still think you can run away from them?

I don't know, I'm pretty fast...

Tornadoes can last a minute or an hour, so it's hard to say how far you'd have to go to outrun it...and they don't always go in a straight line.

The most dangerous thing about tornadoes is that they're throwing so many things into the air, you're mostly in danger of being hit by stuff rather than being picked up by the tornado.

THUNK!

So if there's a tornado warning, you need to get into a room with no windows so nothing can come through and hit you, and preferably get to a basement or something underground where the walls can't be damaged. At the very least, you need to be in the center of your house.

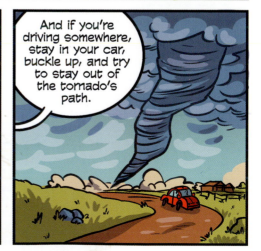

And if you're driving somewhere, stay in your car, buckle up, and try to stay out of the tornado's path.

What about hurricanes? They're not that tough, right?

They might be tougher, actually.

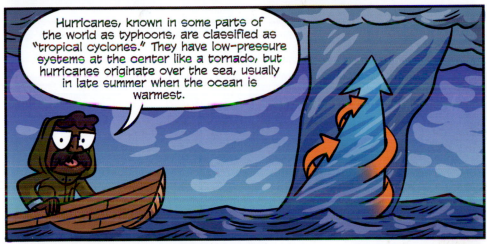

Hurricanes, known in some parts of the world as typhoons, are classified as "tropical cyclones." They have low-pressure systems at the center like a tornado, but hurricanes originate over the sea, usually in late summer when the ocean is warmest.

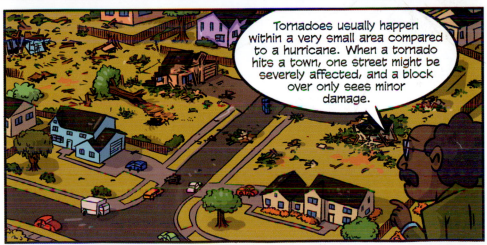

Tornadoes usually happen within a very small area compared to a hurricane. When a tornado hits a town, one street might be severely affected, and a block over only sees minor damage.

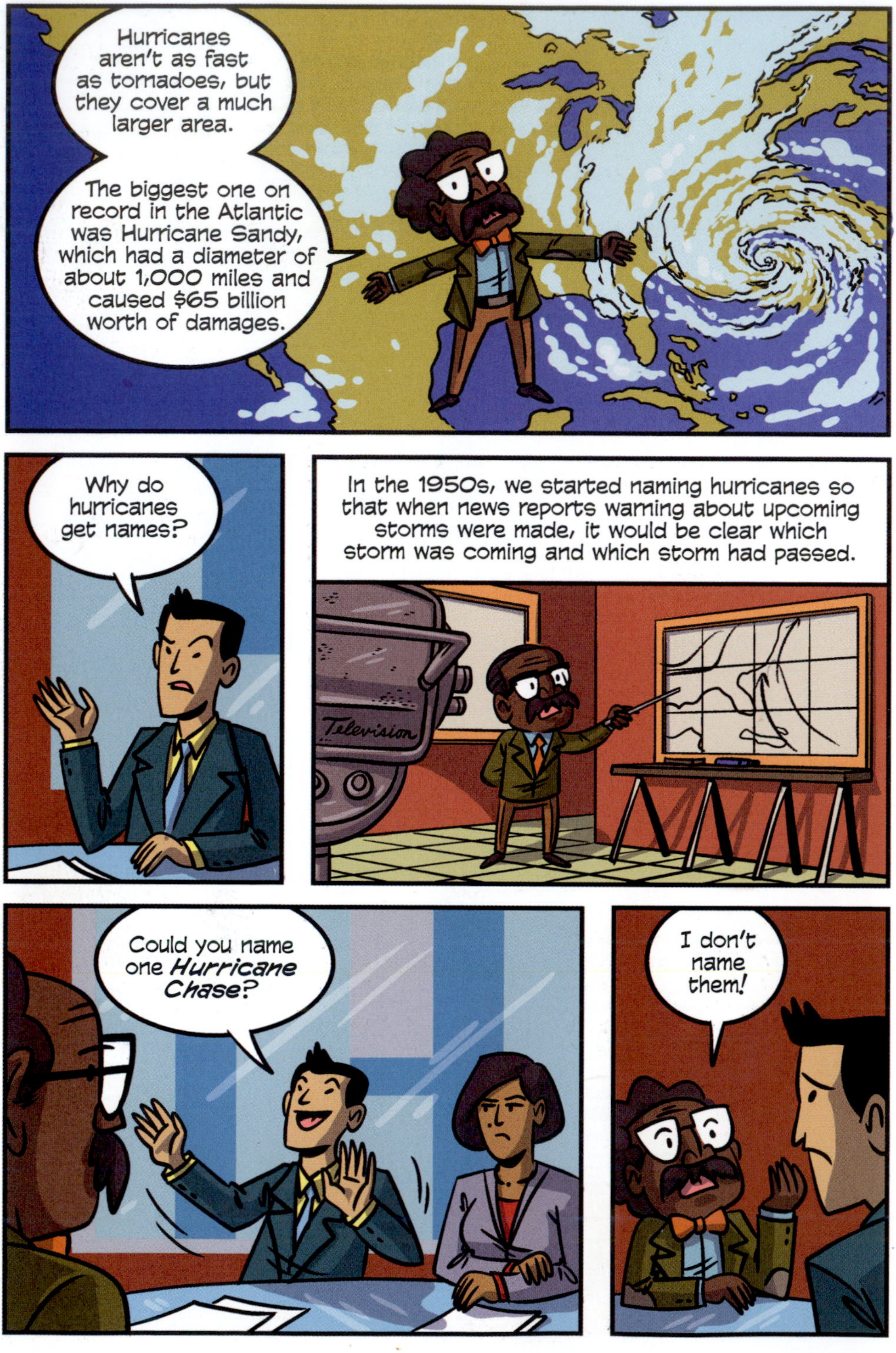
Hurricanes aren't as fast as tornadoes, but they cover a much larger area.
The biggest one on record in the Atlantic was Hurricane Sandy, which had a diameter of about 1,000 miles and caused $65 billion worth of damages.
Why do hurricanes get names?
In the 1950s, we started naming hurricanes so that when news reports warning about upcoming storms were made, it would be clear which storm was coming and which storm had passed.
Television
Could you name one *Hurricane Chase*?
I don't name them!

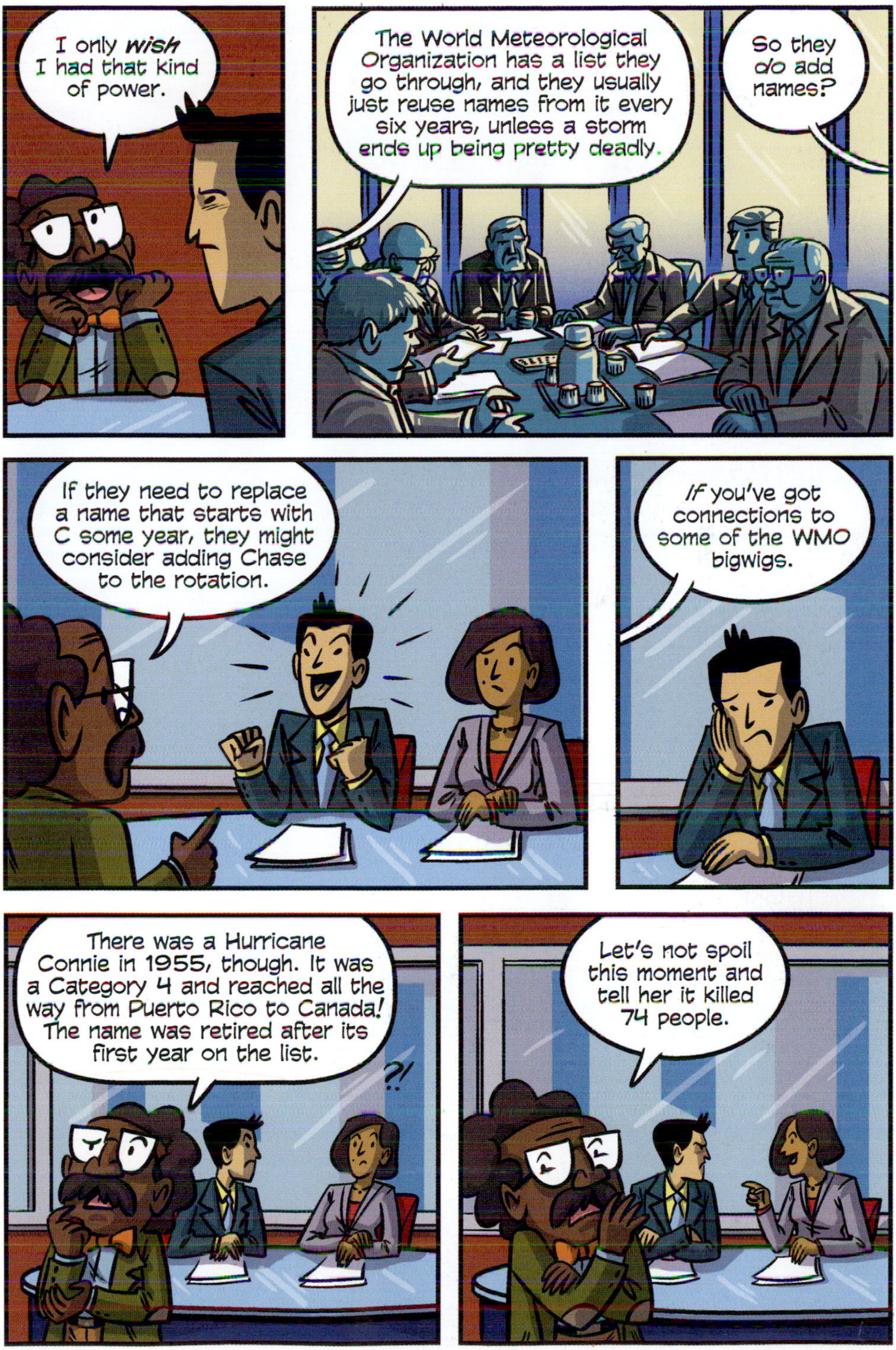
I only *wish* I had that kind of power.
The World Meteorological Organization has a list they go through, and they usually just reuse names from it every six years, unless a storm ends up being pretty deadly.
So they *do* add names?
If they need to replace a name that starts with C some year, they might consider adding Chase to the rotation.
If you've got connections to some of the WMO bigwigs.
There was a Hurricane Connie in 1955, though. It was a Category 4 and reached all the way from Puerto Rico to Canada! The name was retired after its first year on the list.
?!
Let's not spoil this moment and tell her it killed 74 people.

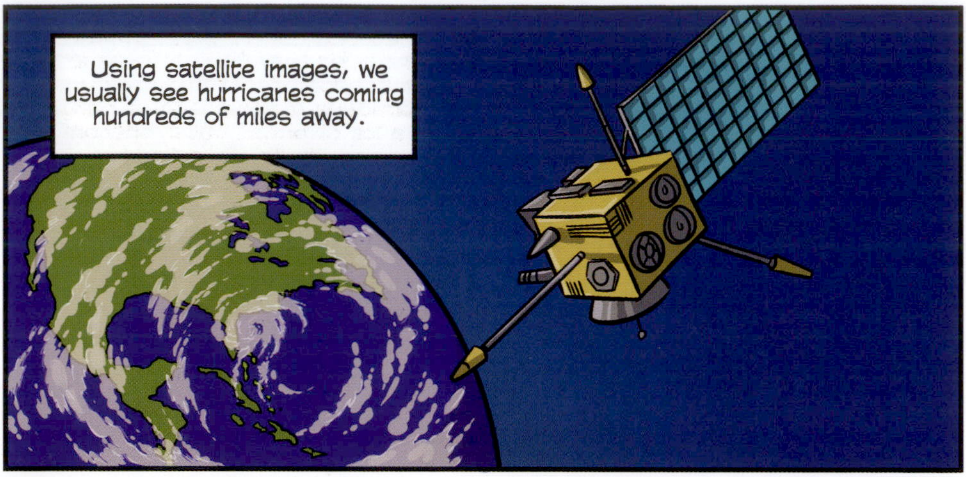
Using satellite images, we usually see hurricanes coming hundreds of miles away.

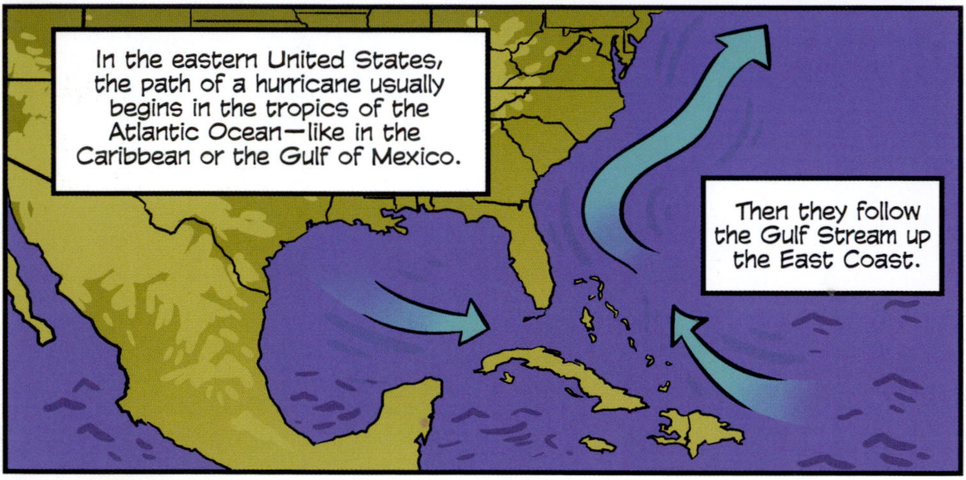
In the eastern United States, the path of a hurricane usually begins in the tropics of the Atlantic Ocean—like in the Caribbean or the Gulf of Mexico.
Then they follow the Gulf Stream up the East Coast.

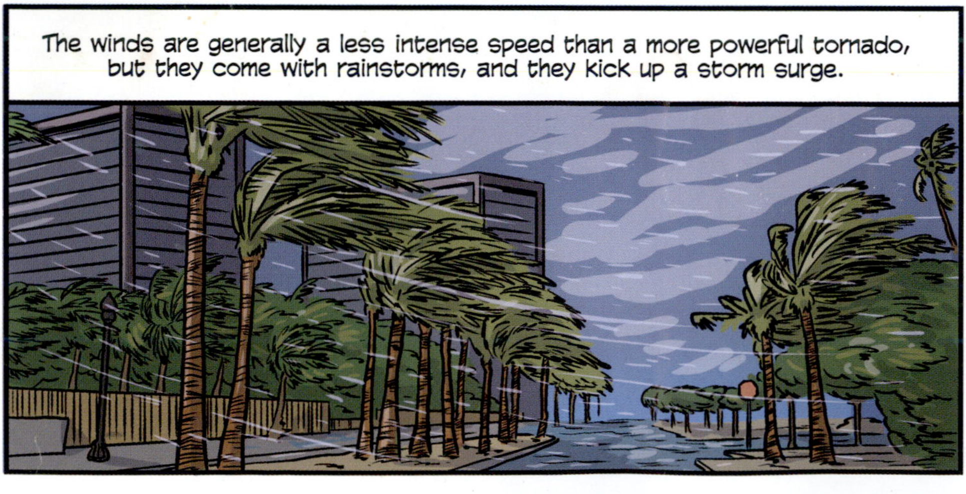
The winds are generally a less intense speed than a more powerful tornado, but they come with rainstorms, and they kick up a storm surge.

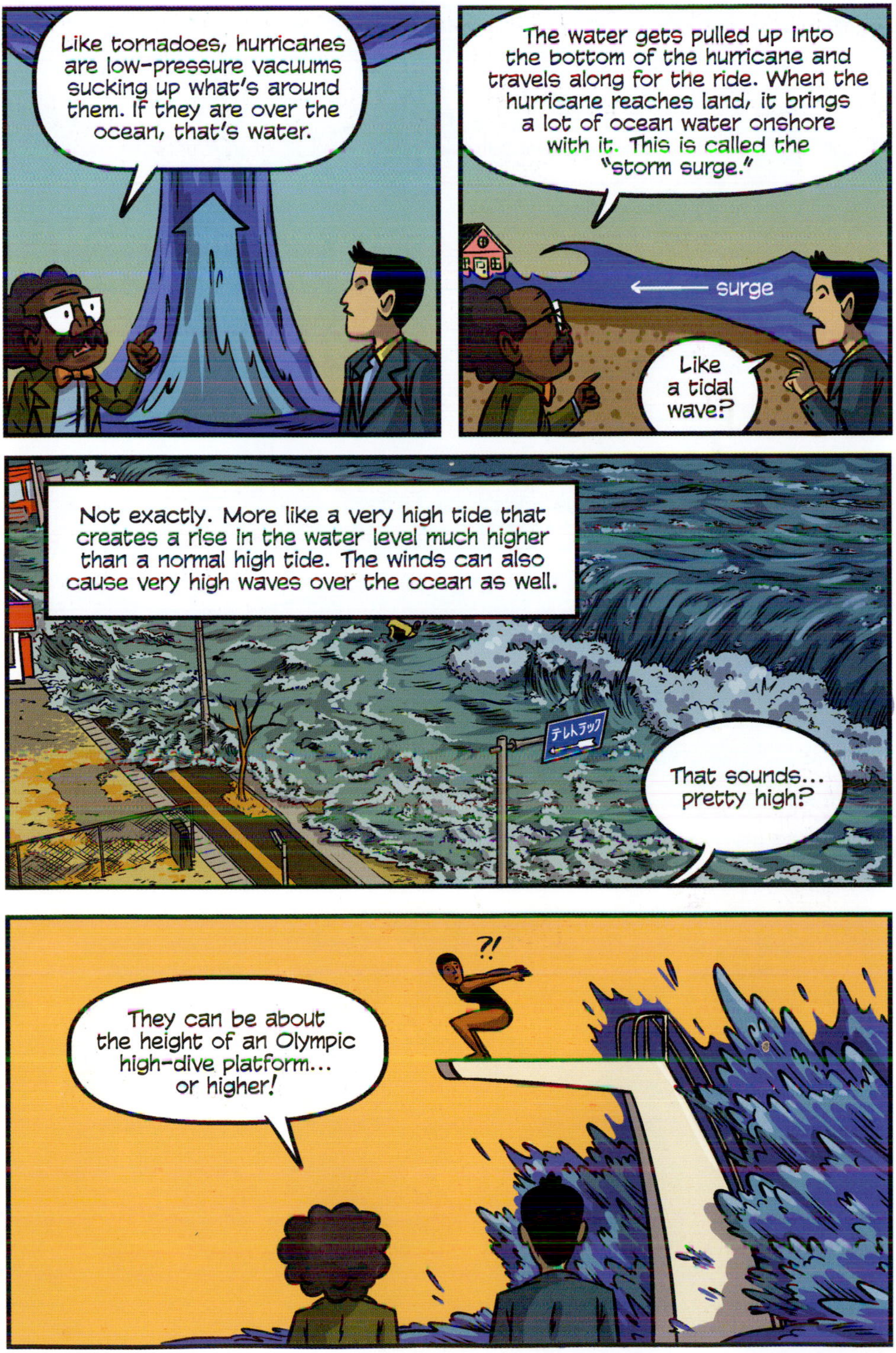
Like tornadoes, hurricanes are low-pressure vacuums sucking up what's around them. If they are over the ocean, that's water.
The water gets pulled up into the bottom of the hurricane and travels along for the ride. When the hurricane reaches land, it brings a lot of ocean water onshore with it. This is called the "storm surge."
surge
Like a tidal wave?
Not exactly. More like a very high tide that creates a rise in the water level much higher than a normal high tide. The winds can also cause very high waves over the ocean as well.
テレトラック
That sounds... pretty high?
?!
They can be about the height of an Olympic high-dive platform... or higher!

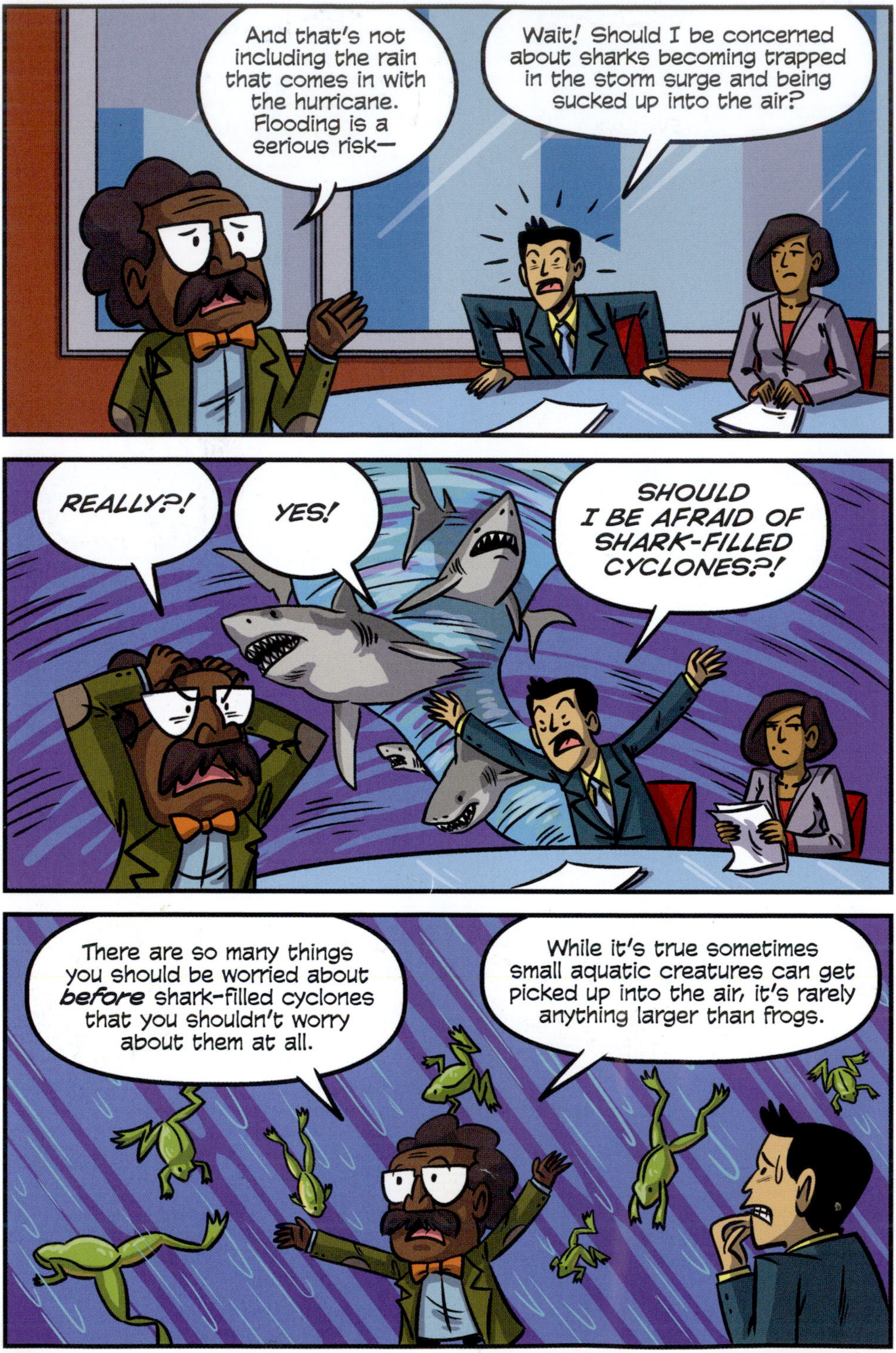
And that's not including the rain that comes in with the hurricane. Flooding is a serious risk—
Wait! Should I be concerned about sharks becoming trapped in the storm surge and being sucked up into the air?
REALLY?!
YES!
SHOULD I BE AFRAID OF SHARK-FILLED CYCLONES?!
There are so many things you should be worried about *before* shark-filled cyclones that you shouldn't worry about them at all.
While it's true sometimes small aquatic creatures can get picked up into the air, it's rarely anything larger than frogs.

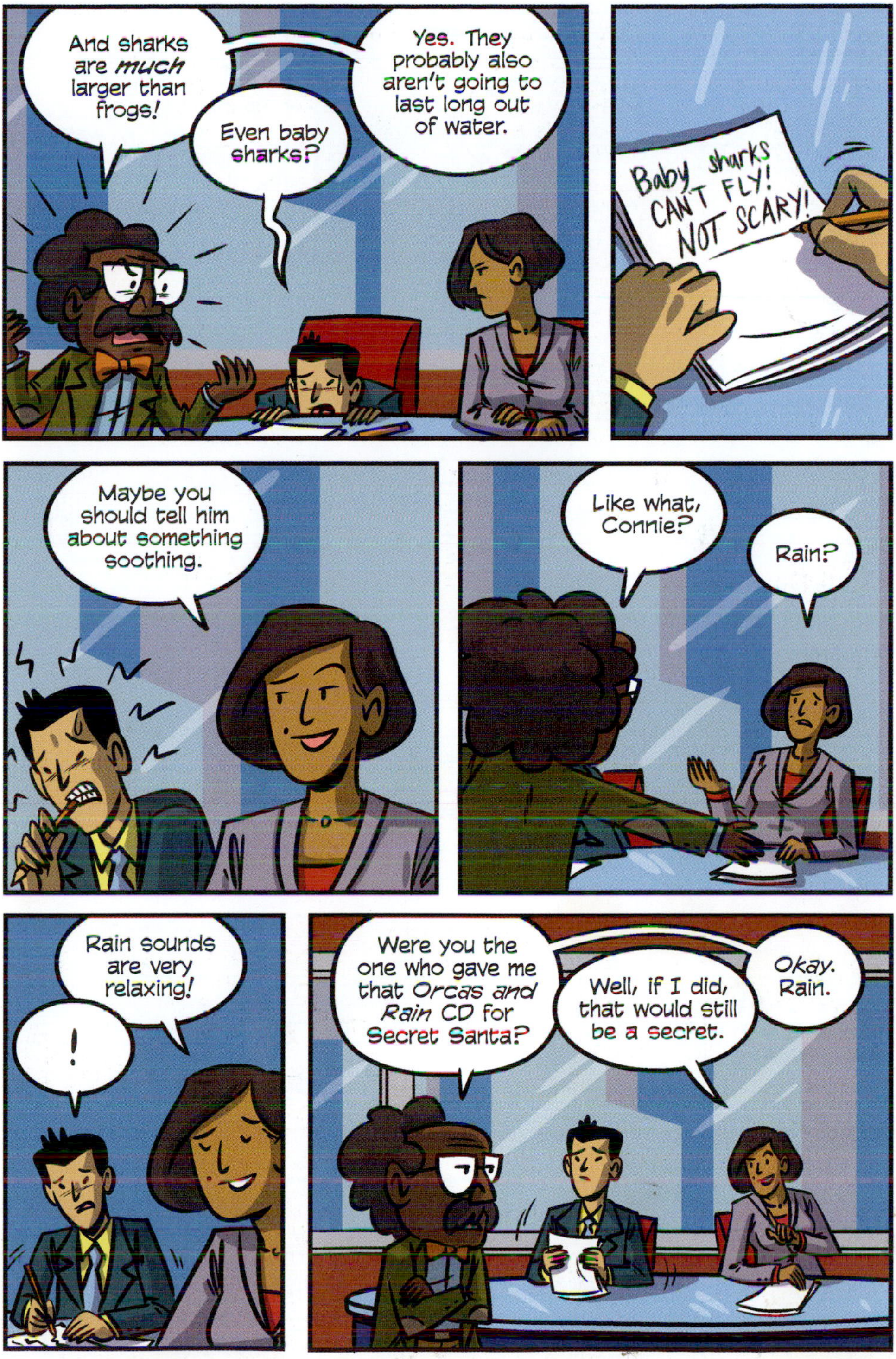
And sharks are *much* larger than frogs!
Even baby sharks?
Yes. They probably also aren't going to last long out of water.
Baby sharks CAN'T FLY! NOT SCARY!
Maybe you should tell him about something soothing.
Like what, Connie?
Rain?
Rain sounds are very relaxing!
!
Were you the one who gave me that *Orcas and Rain* CD for Secret Santa?
Well, if I did, that would still be a secret.
Okay. Rain.

To get rain, we need to talk about the water cycle and water vapor.

What is that again?

It's the gaseous state of water, when the individual water molecules are not bonded, or stuck together. The water cycle is a loop that works like this...

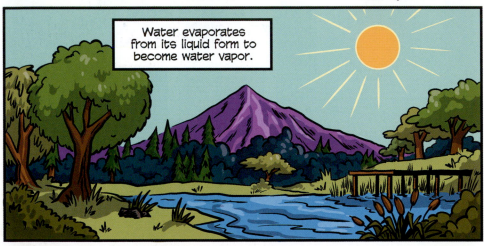

Water evaporates from its liquid form to become water vapor.

It rises with warm air.

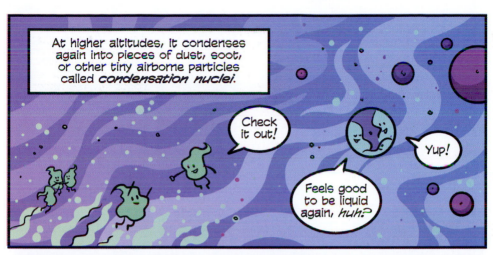

At higher altitudes, it condenses again into pieces of dust, soot, or other tiny airborne particles called *condensation nuclei*.

Check it out!

Yup!

Feels good to be liquid again, *huh?*

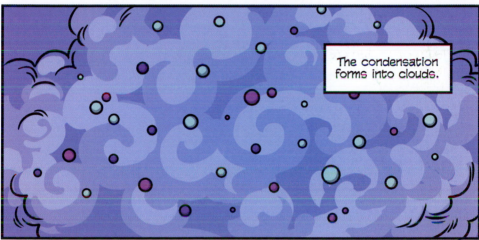

The condensation forms into clouds.

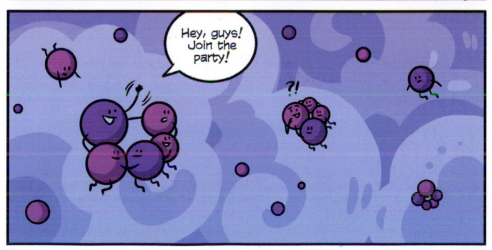

Hey, guys! Join the party!

?!

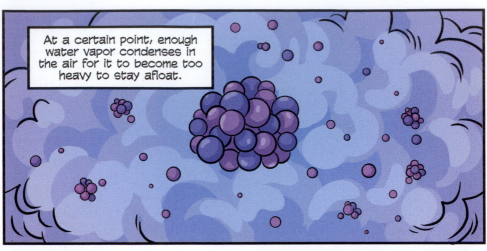

At a certain point, enough water vapor condenses in the air for it to become too heavy to stay afloat.

Uh, guys, I feel funny...

Then it is called *precipitation*.

And that is?

Water that falls from the clouds in any number of forms, like rain, snow, sleet, or hail.

After it rains, water is reabsorbed back into the cycle. It might go over land into streams and rivers and lakes.

Plants will grab what they can to feed themselves, and give off some water vapor again as a gas, through *transpiration*.

When it ends up in rivers and lakes, humans and other animals can drink it.

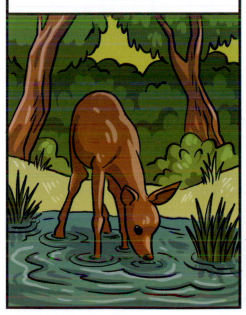

And some of that water will be absorbed into the ground and go underground to fill up permeable rock layers called aquifers.

The water on the surface eventually evaporates, beginning the cycle all over again.

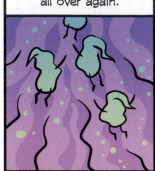

What about snow? It just sits there.

Snow will usually stay put until it gets warm enough to melt.

It also reflects the Sun's energy away from the Earth, keeping the surface colder.

In some areas, like on tall mountains or near the poles, snow doesn't melt. It builds up and eventually compresses into ice.

When climatologists take ice core samples from these regions, we can analyze them and determine from bubbles that are trapped in the ice what was in the air years ago.

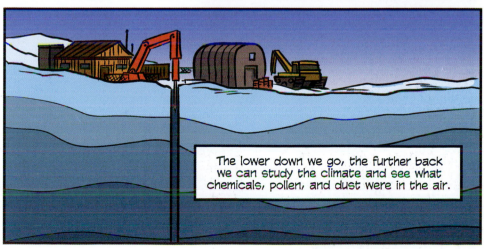

The lower down we go, the further back we can study the climate and see what chemicals, pollen, and dust were in the air.

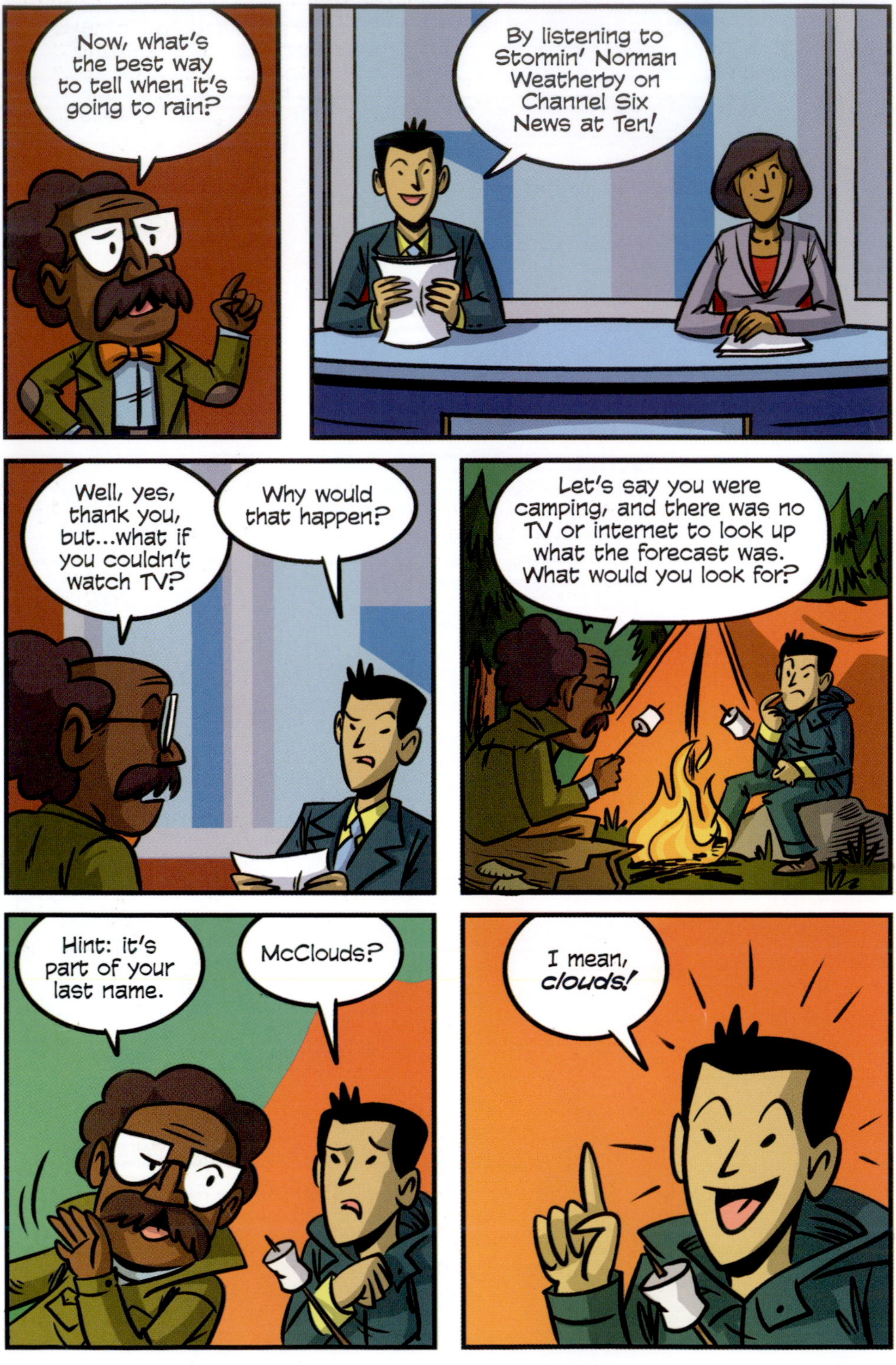
Now, what's the best way to tell when it's going to rain?
By listening to Stormin' Norman Weatherby on Channel Six News at Ten!
Well, yes, thank you, but...what if you couldn't watch TV?
Why would that happen?
Let's say you were camping, and there was no TV or internet to look up what the forecast was. What would you look for?
Hint: it's part of your last name.
McClouds?
I mean, *clouds!*

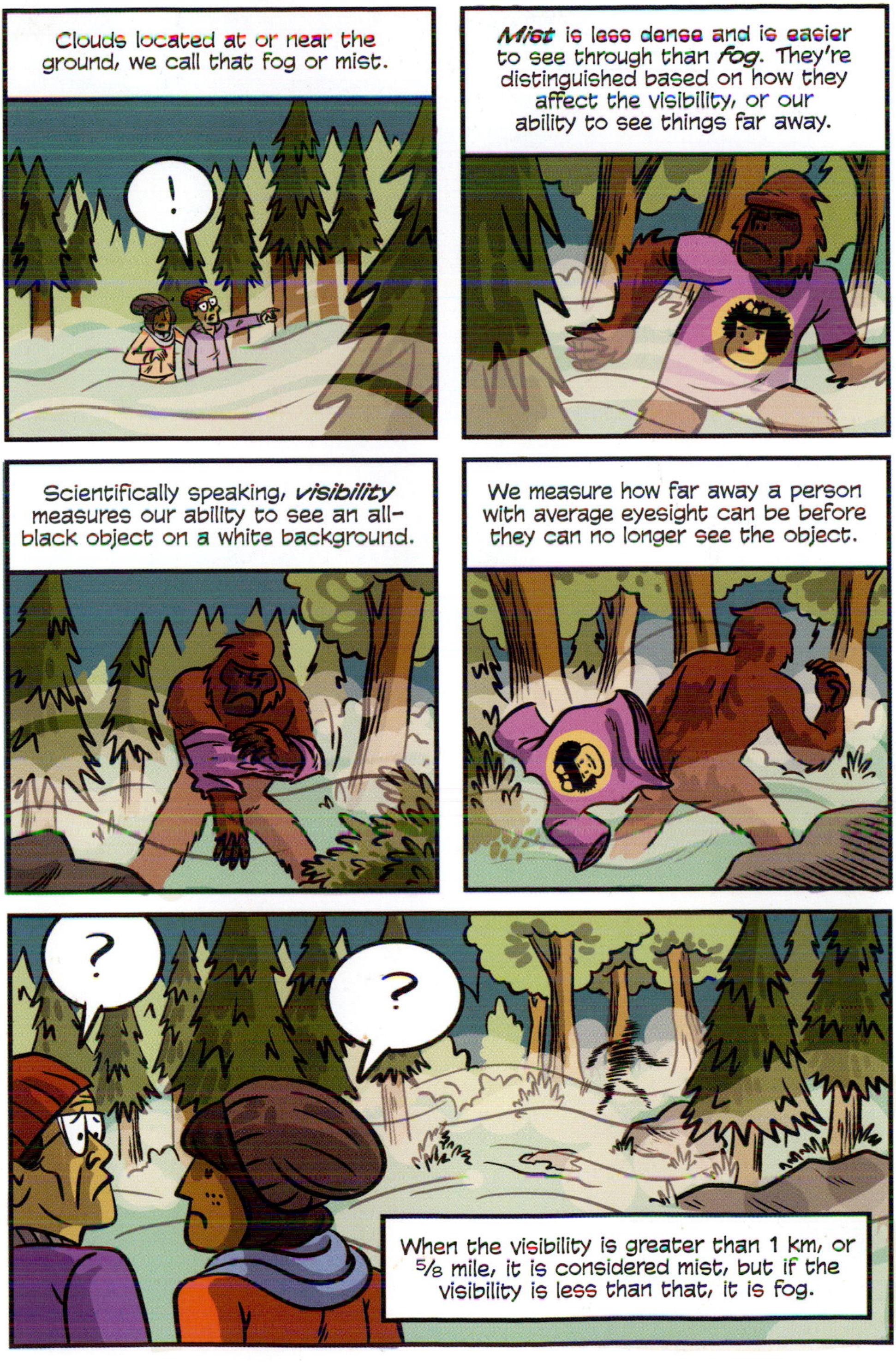

Clouds located at or near the ground, we call that fog or mist.
!
Mist is less dense and is easier to see through than *fog*. They're distinguished based on how they affect the visibility, or our ability to see things far away.
Scientifically speaking, *visibility* measures our ability to see an all-black object on a white background.
We measure how far away a person with average eyesight can be before they can no longer see the object.
?
?
When the visibility is greater than 1 km, or 5/8 mile, it is considered mist, but if the visibility is less than that, it is fog.

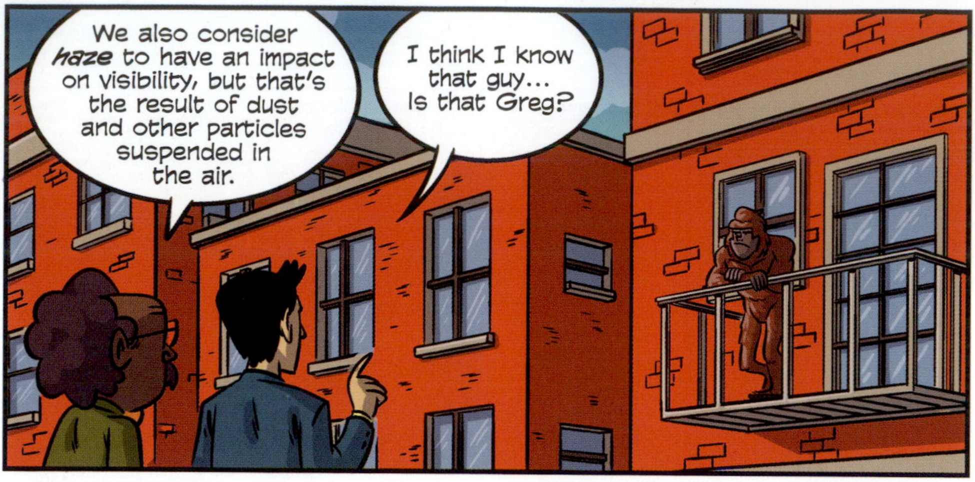
We also consider *haze* to have an impact on visibility, but that's the result of dust and other particles suspended in the air.
I think I know that guy... Is that Greg?

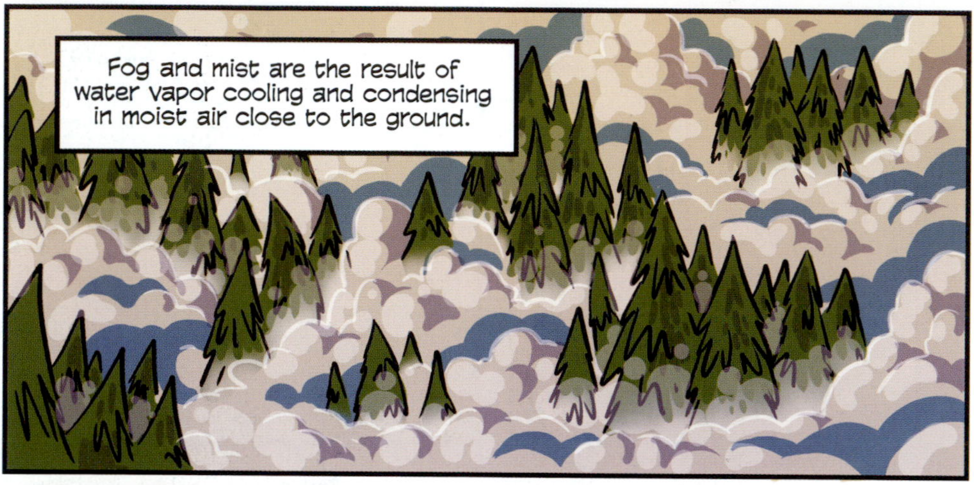
Fog and mist are the result of water vapor cooling and condensing in moist air close to the ground.

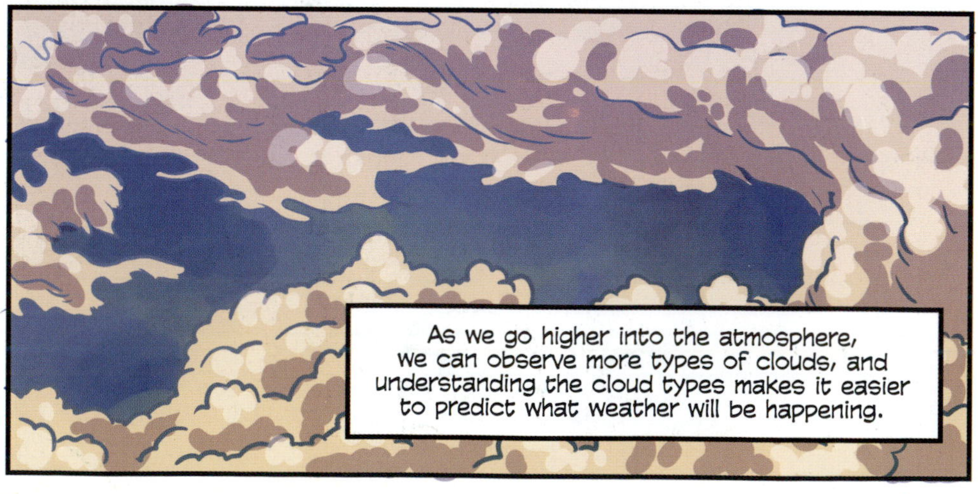
As we go higher into the atmosphere, we can observe more types of clouds, and understanding the cloud types makes it easier to predict what weather will be happening.

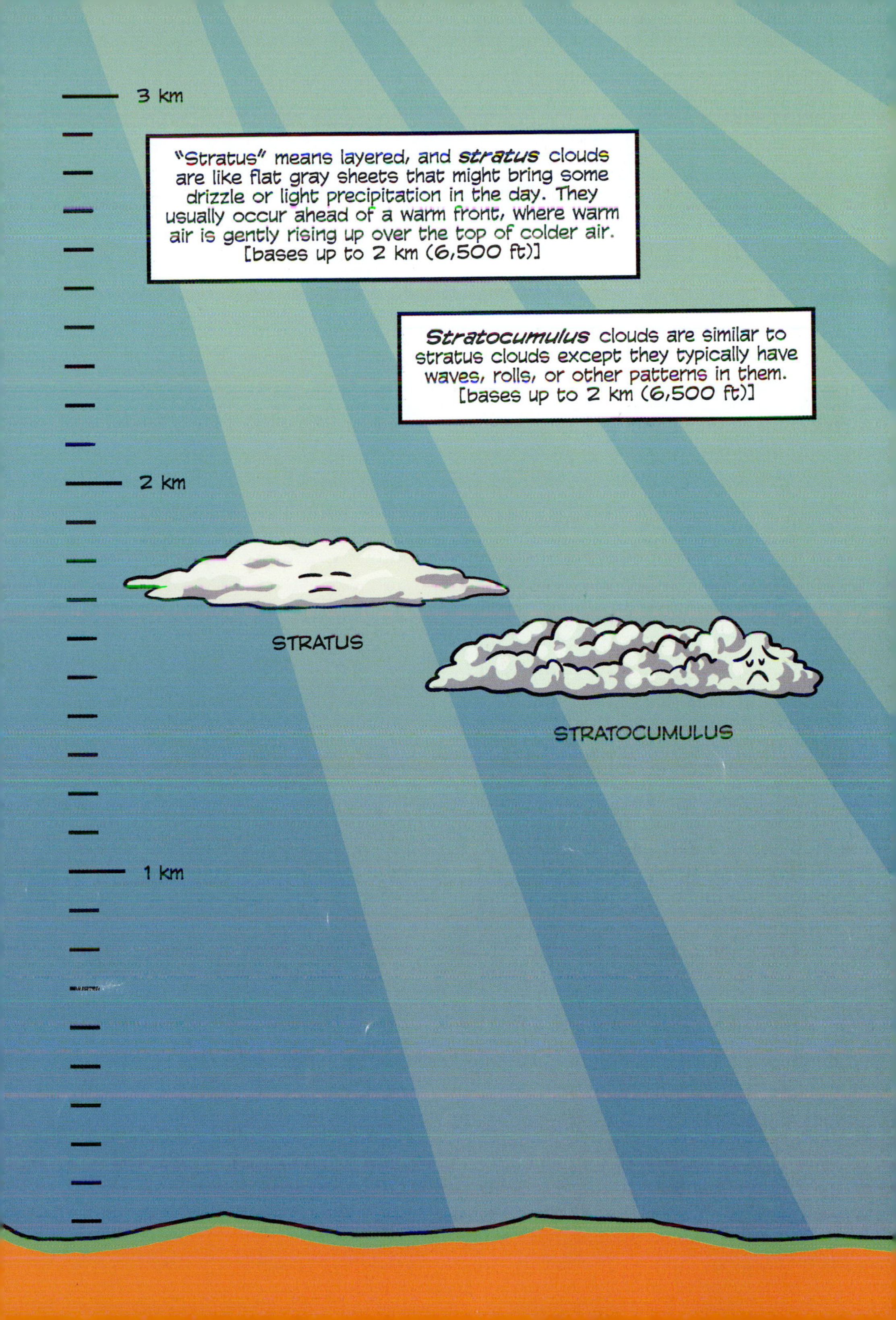
3 km
"Stratus" means layered, and *stratus* clouds are like flat gray sheets that might bring some drizzle or light precipitation in the day. They usually occur ahead of a warm front, where warm air is gently rising up over the top of colder air. [bases up to 2 km (6,500 ft)]
Stratocumulus clouds are similar to stratus clouds except they typically have waves, rolls, or other patterns in them. [bases up to 2 km (6,500 ft)]
2 km
STRATUS
STRATOCUMULUS
1 km

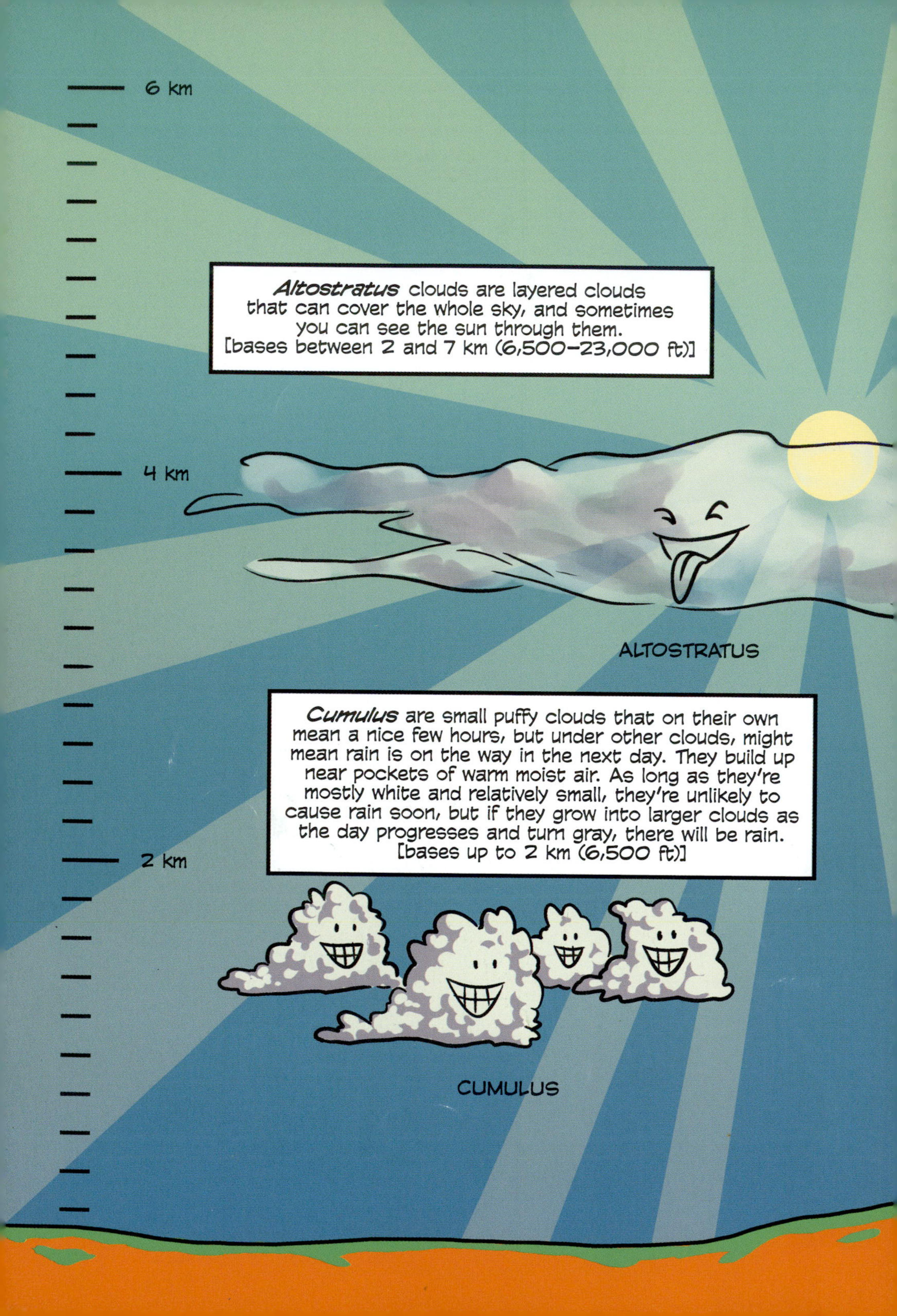
6 km
Altostratus clouds are layered clouds that can cover the whole sky, and sometimes you can see the sun through them. [bases between 2 and 7 km (6,500–23,000 ft)]
4 km
ALTOSTRATUS
Cumulus are small puffy clouds that on their own mean a nice few hours, but under other clouds, might mean rain is on the way in the next day. They build up near pockets of warm moist air. As long as they're mostly white and relatively small, they're unlikely to cause rain soon, but if they grow into larger clouds as the day progresses and turn gray, there will be rain. [bases up to 2 km (6,500 ft)]
2 km
CUMULUS

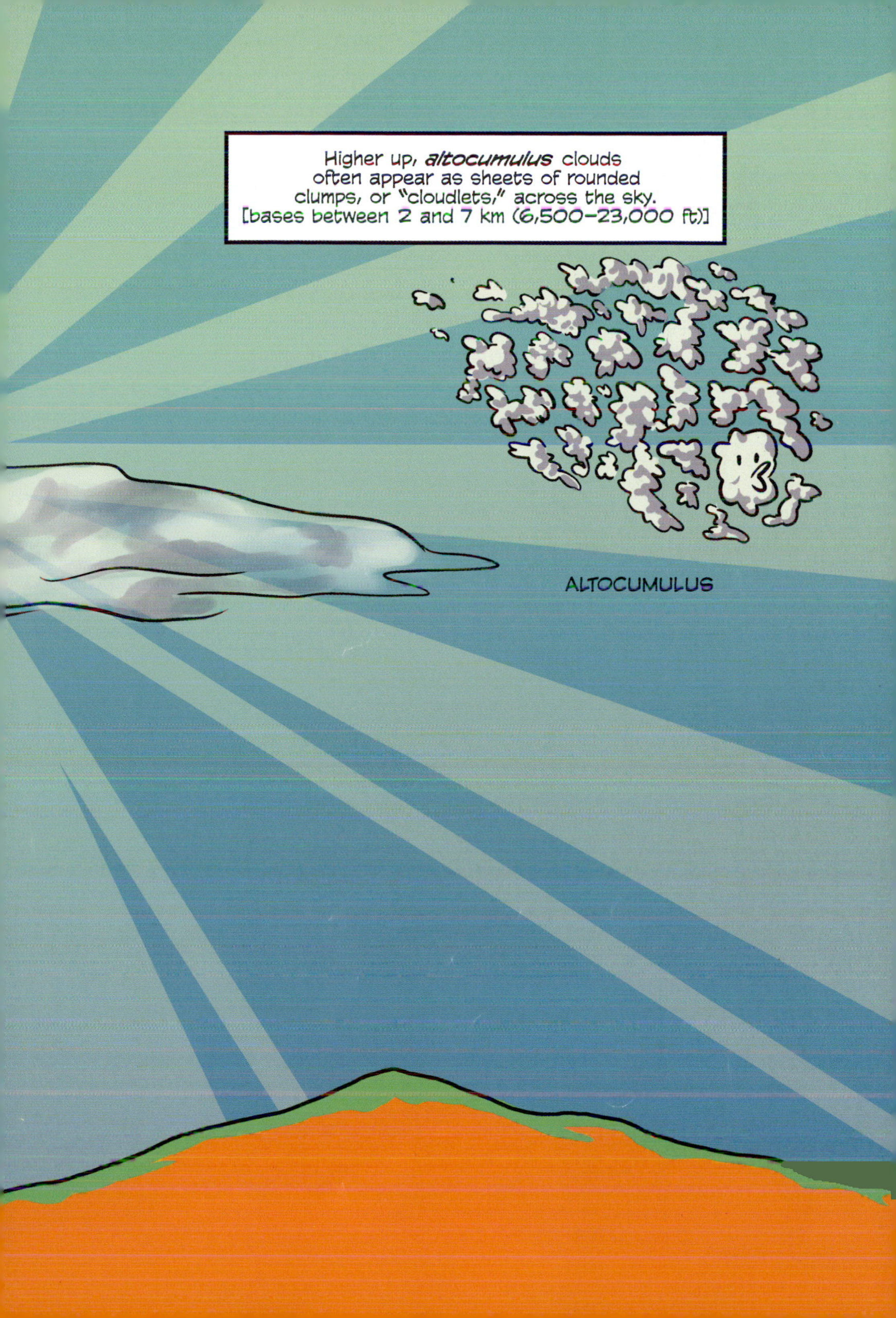
Higher up, *altocumulus* clouds often appear as sheets of rounded clumps, or "cloudlets," across the sky. [bases between 2 and 7 km (6,500–23,000 ft)]
ALTOCUMULUS

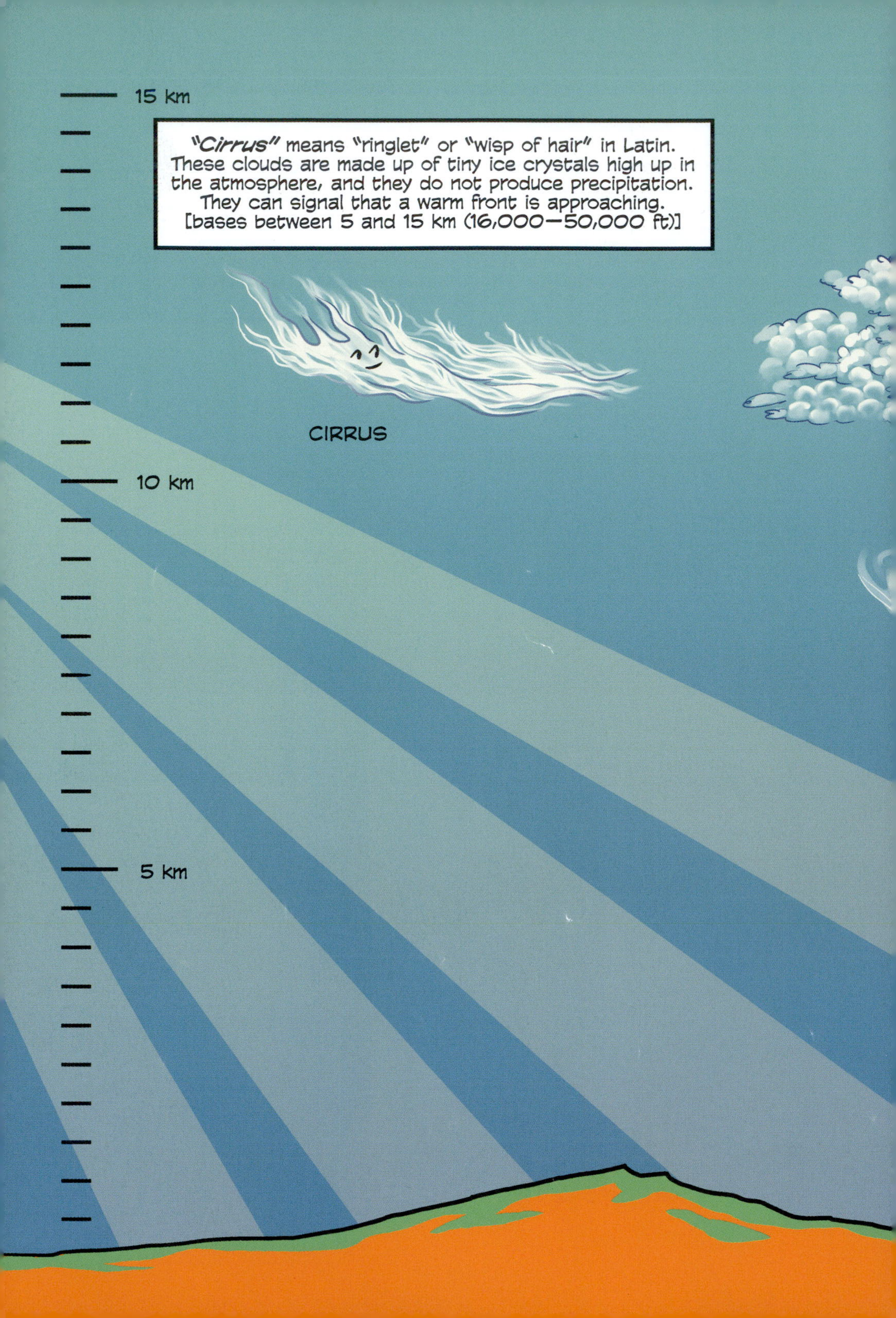
15 km
"Cirrus" means "ringlet" or "wisp of hair" in Latin. These clouds are made up of tiny ice crystals high up in the atmosphere, and they do not produce precipitation. They can signal that a warm front is approaching. [bases between 5 and 15 km (16,000—50,000 ft)]
CIRRUS
10 km
5 km

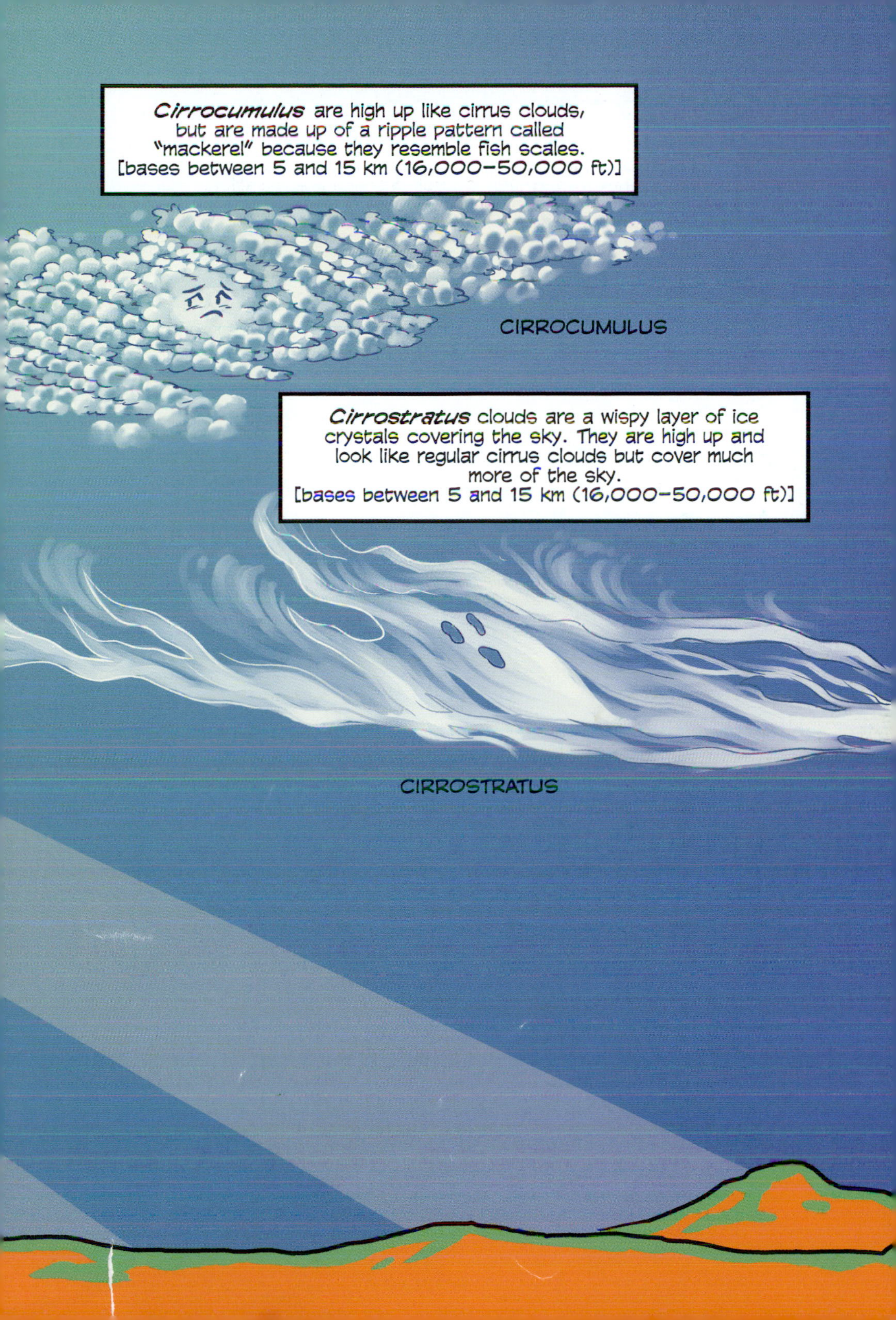
Cirrocumulus are high up like cirrus clouds, but are made up of a ripple pattern called "mackerel" because they resemble fish scales. [bases between 5 and 15 km (16,000–50,000 ft)]
CIRROCUMULUS
Cirrostratus clouds are a wispy layer of ice crystals covering the sky. They are high up and look like regular cirrus clouds but cover much more of the sky. [bases between 5 and 15 km (16,000–50,000 ft)]
CIRROSTRATUS

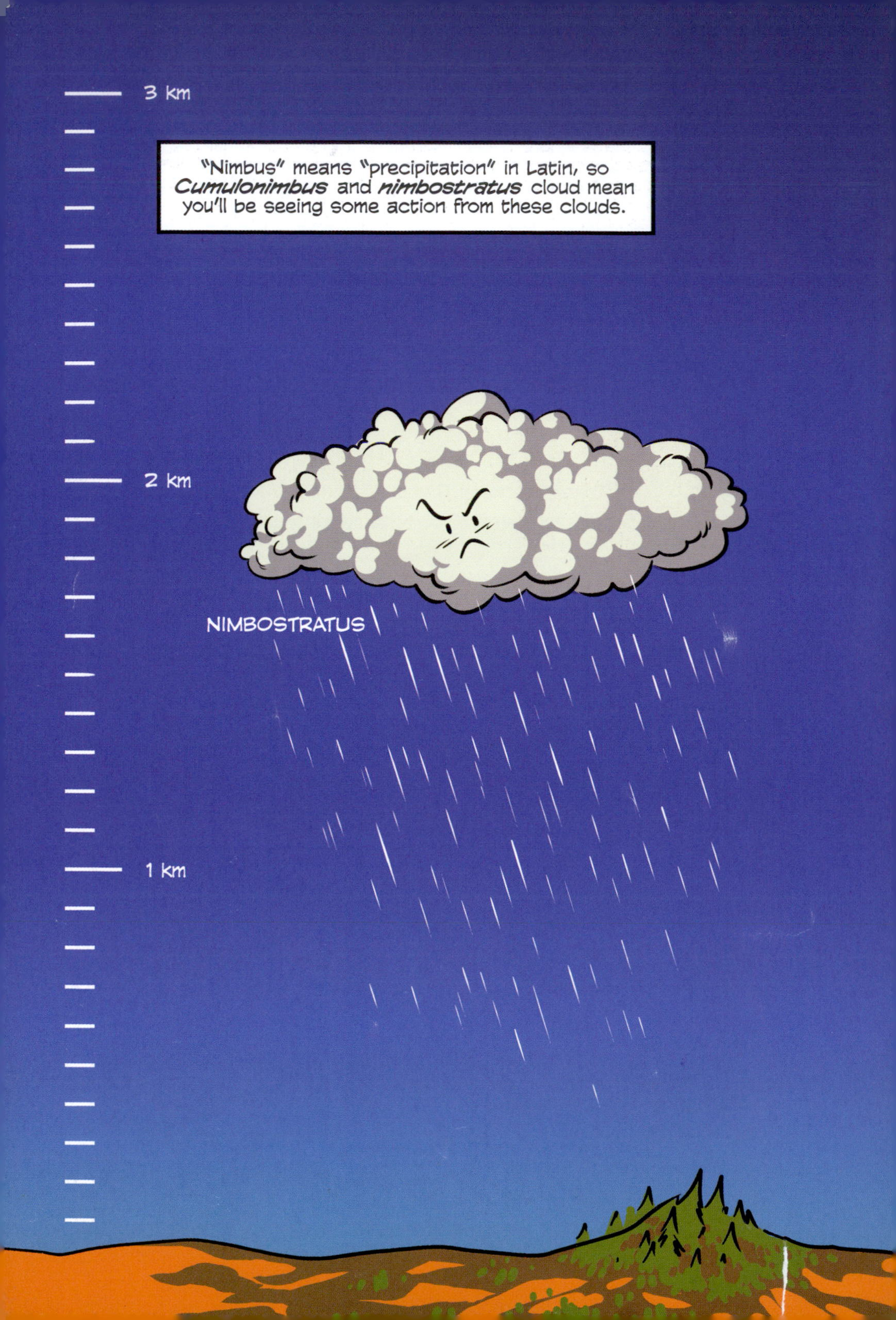
3 km
"Nimbus" means "precipitation" in Latin, so *Cumulonimbus* and *nimbostratus* cloud mean you'll be seeing some action from these clouds.
2 km
NIMBOSTRATUS
1 km

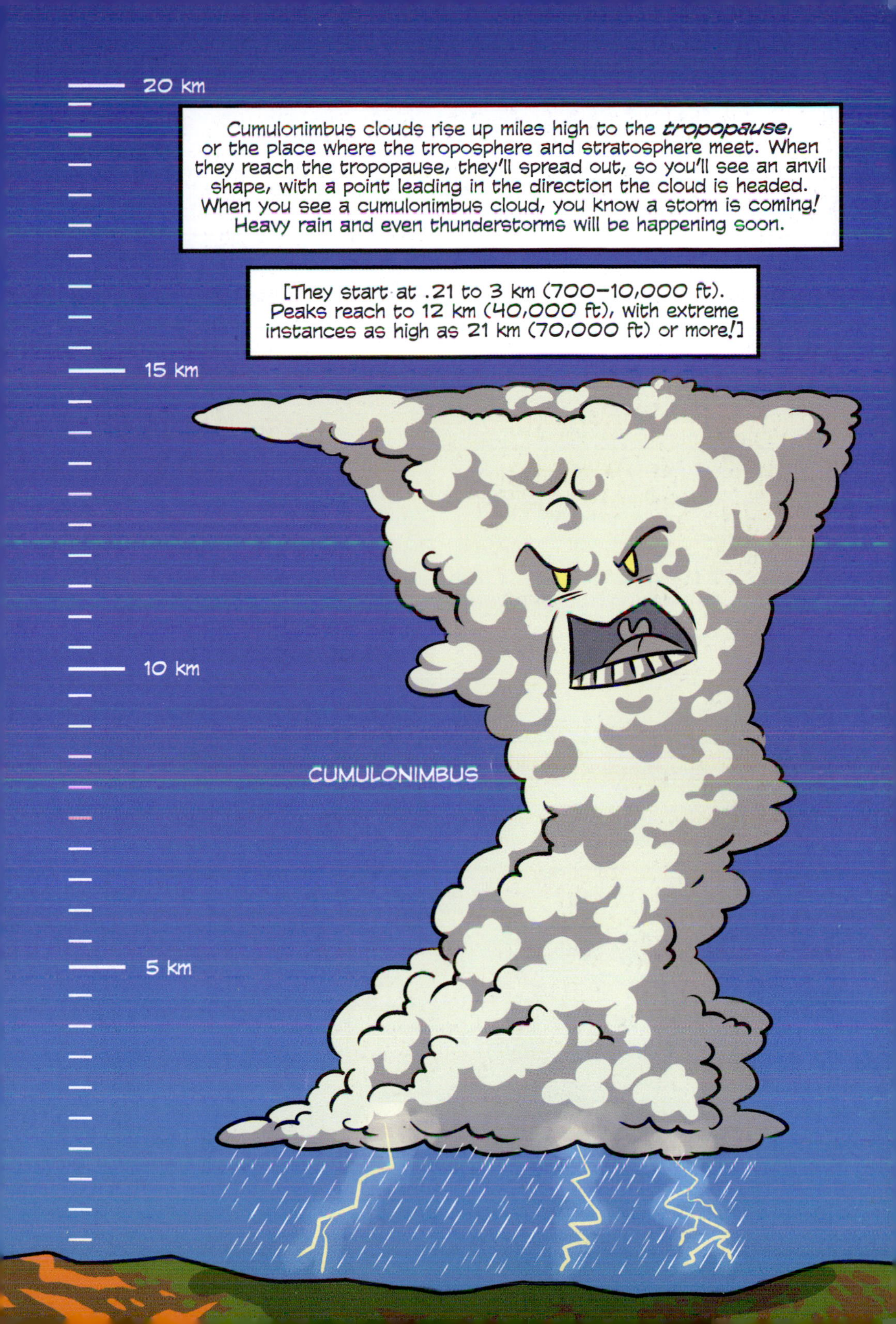
20 km
Cumulonimbus clouds rise up miles high to the *tropopause*, or the place where the troposphere and stratosphere meet. When they reach the tropopause, they'll spread out, so you'll see an anvil shape, with a point leading in the direction the cloud is headed. When you see a cumulonimbus cloud, you know a storm is coming! Heavy rain and even thunderstorms will be happening soon.
[They start at .21 to 3 km (700–10,000 ft). Peaks reach to 12 km (40,000 ft), with extreme instances as high as 21 km (70,000 ft) or more!]
15 km
10 km
CUMULONIMBUS
5 km

In the right conditions, clouds might release their water only to have it evaporate before it hits the ground. This is called *virga*. It can occur when the air is very dry, such as in an arid region like the desert.

But why did you keep saying "precipitation," just before? I think you're trying to sound fancy. Just say "rain," Norman! Like a normal person!

But it might not be rain, Chase! Depending on what's happening in that cloud, you might get sleet, hail, or snow.

They're all forms of frozen or partially frozen water.

A lot can happen to a water molecule between its formation in the clouds and the trip down to Earth.

, Drizzle	• Rain	✳ Snow
◬ Sleet	△ Hail	℞ Thunder-storm

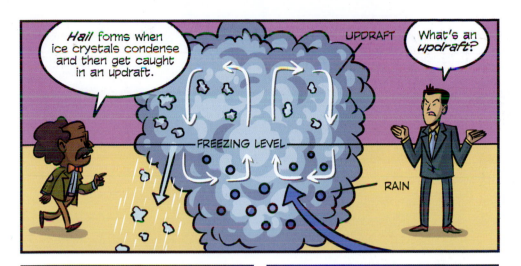

Hail forms when ice crystals condense and then get caught in an updraft.
UPDRAFT
What's an updraft?
FREEZING LEVEL
RAIN
It's a warmer part of air within the cloud that pushes precipitation back upward. So hail goes through the place where ice is condensing again and grows bigger each time it passes through.
FREEZING LEVEL
Sometimes hail particles rise and fall many times in updrafts and downdrafts, and then it can get quite large before it gets heavy enough to fall.
Usually we talk about the size of hail as being pea-sized or golf-ball-sized, but sometimes hail can get up to baseball- or grapefruit-sized pieces.
Bro!
They're not actually perfectly spherical like a ball, but that puts it in terms people can easily visualize, rather than saying, "It had a nine-inch diameter!"

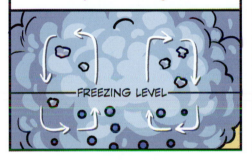

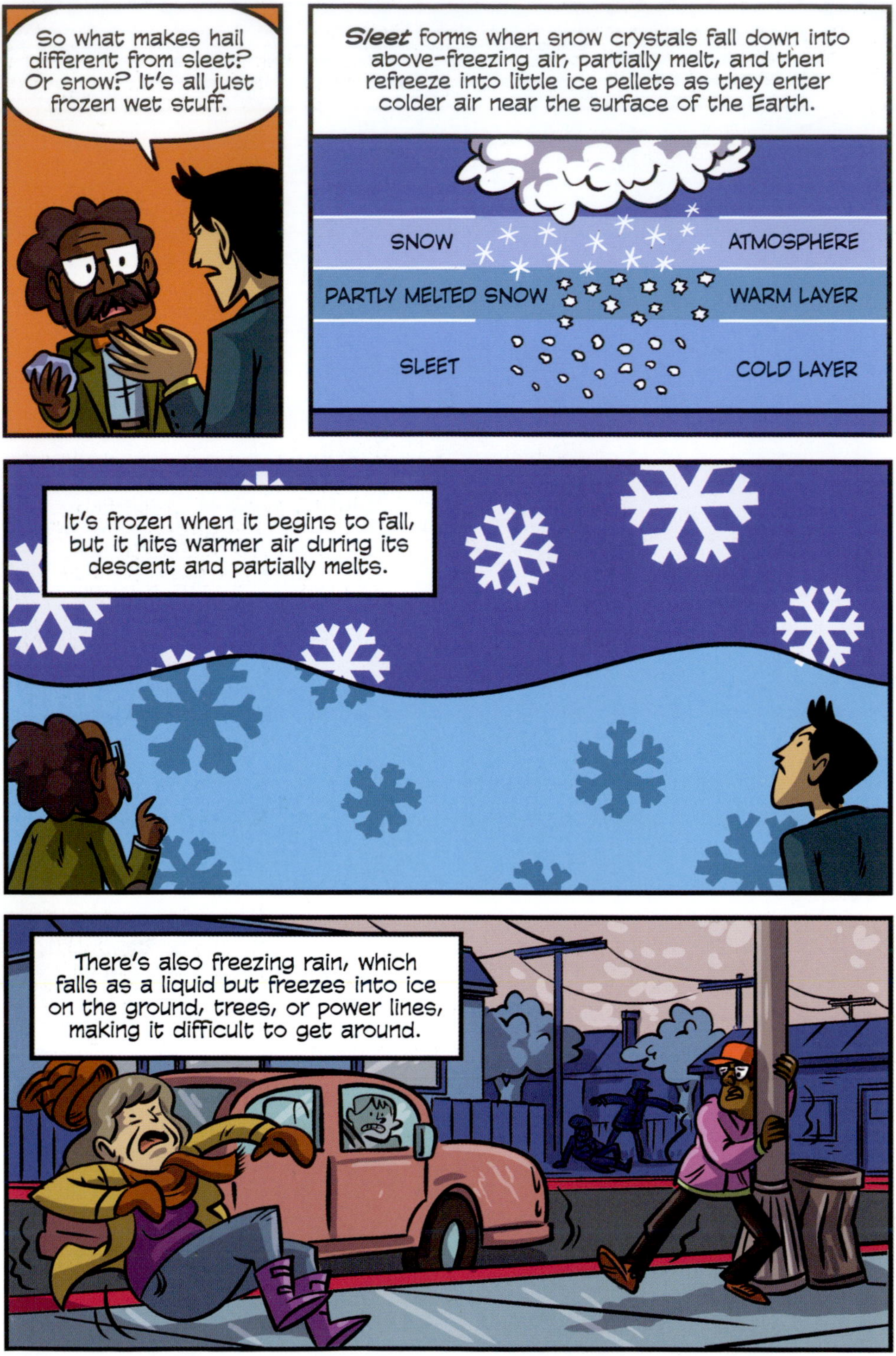
So what makes hail different from sleet? Or snow? It's all just frozen wet stuff.
Sleet forms when snow crystals fall down into above-freezing air, partially melt, and then refreeze into little ice pellets as they enter colder air near the surface of the Earth.
SNOW
ATMOSPHERE
PARTLY MELTED SNOW
WARM LAYER
SLEET
COLD LAYER
It's frozen when it begins to fall, but it hits warmer air during its descent and partially melts.
There's also freezing rain, which falls as a liquid but freezes into ice on the ground, trees, or power lines, making it difficult to get around.

Snow is crystalized water vapor.

It forms when water vapor in the air is super cooled, and stays cold for its whole descent.

Norman, what about blizzards? Will SNOWPOCALYPSE be considered one?

SNOWPOCALYPSE 20XX

To qualify, Snowpocalypse would have to hit sustained wind speeds of 35 mph or higher, steadily or in regular gusts, and the visibility would have to be reduced to ¼ of a mile for at least 3 hours.

SPEED LIMIT 35

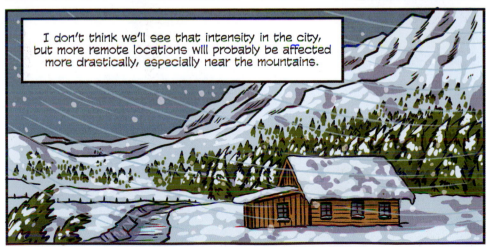

I don't think we'll see that intensity in the city, but more remote locations will probably be affected more drastically, especially near the mountains.

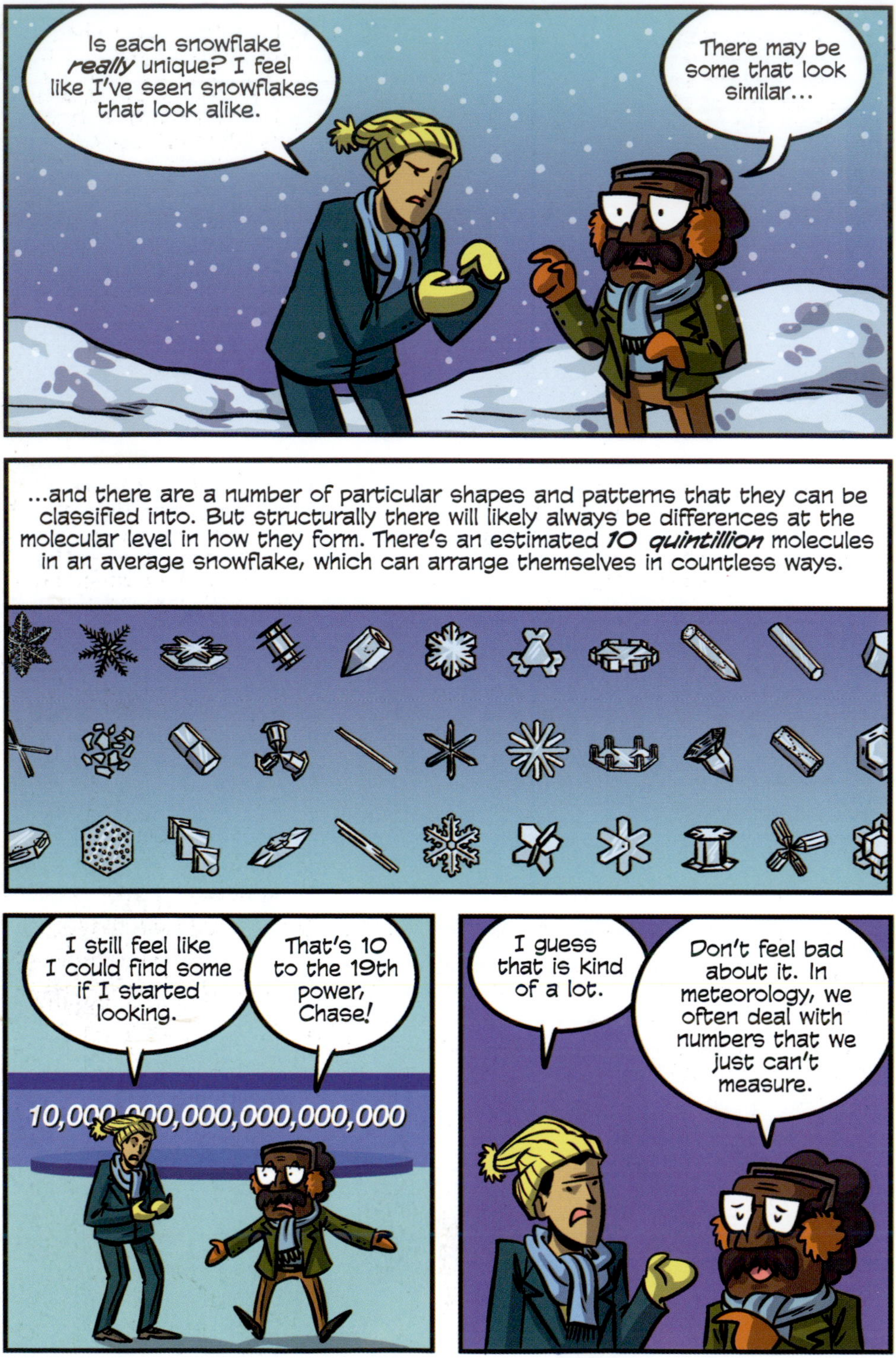
Is each snowflake *really* unique? I feel like I've seen snowflakes that look alike.
There may be some that look similar...
...and there are a number of particular shapes and patterns that they can be classified into. But structurally there will likely always be differences at the molecular level in how they form. There's an estimated ***10 quintillion*** molecules in an average snowflake, which can arrange themselves in countless ways.
I still feel like I could find some if I started looking.
That's 10 to the 19th power, Chase!
10,000,000,000,000,000,000
I guess that is kind of a lot.
Don't feel bad about it. In meteorology, we often deal with numbers that we just can't measure.

It's a challenge to predict specifically what's going to happen that accurately over a long period of time because there are too many variables to measure.

Why?

You can tell pretty broadly what's going to happen tomorrow over a certain area, but it's hard to predict *precisely*. The further out in time the forecast goes, the harder it is to predict exactly what will happen. Tiny errors in measurements multiply over time, which can send a computer forecast off the rails.

I can tell you it should snow between 6 and 12 inches tomorrow, but I can't tell you exactly how much because I can't measure how much condensation is in the cloud or know how microclimates within the city are going to affect the snow.

WED	THU	FRI	SAT	SUN
❄❄❄ ❄❄❄ ❄❄❄	❄❄❄ ❄❄❄ ❄❄❄	❄❄ ❄❄	☀	☀
6"–12"	6"–12"	4"–8"		

Since I can't measure that, I don't have the data to predict what the effects of tomorrow will have on the coming weather of next week.

A really good example of randomness in action is lightning! It's *highly* unpredictable.

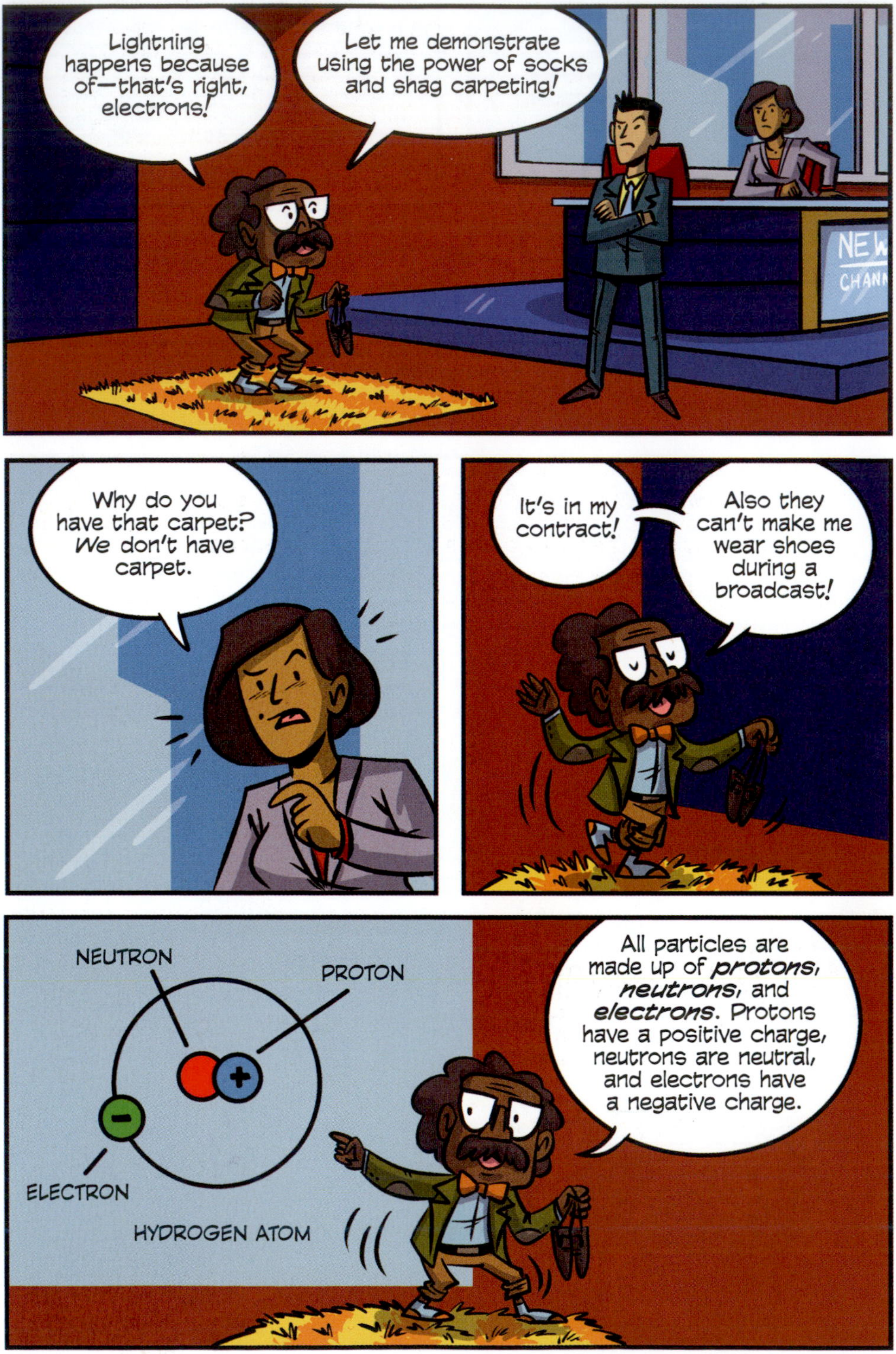
Lightning happens because of—that's right, electrons!
Let me demonstrate using the power of socks and shag carpeting!
NEW
CHANN
Why do you have that carpet? *We* don't have carpet.
It's in my contract!
Also they can't make me wear shoes during a broadcast!
NEUTRON
PROTON
ELECTRON
HYDROGEN ATOM
All particles are made up of ***protons***, ***neutrons***, and ***electrons***. Protons have a positive charge, neutrons are neutral, and electrons have a negative charge.

Like magnets?

Exactly!

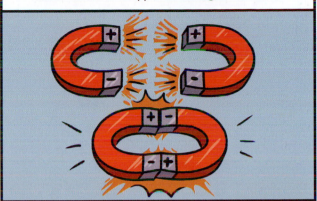

As with magnets, like charges repel each other, and opposite charges attract!

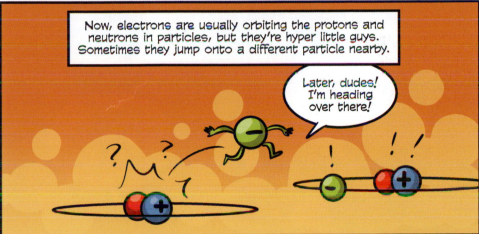

Now, electrons are usually orbiting the protons and neutrons in particles, but they're hyper little guys. Sometimes they jump onto a different particle nearby.

Later, dudes! I'm heading over there!

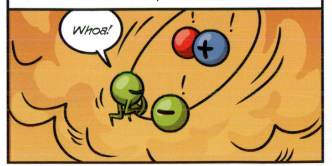

That particle with an extra electron is now negatively charged and ever so slightly heavier. It sinks to the bottom of the cloud. The particle that lost it is positively charged and rises to the top of a cloud.

Whoa!

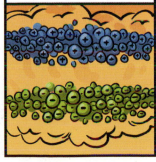

The charges build up, and when there's enough to overcome the insulation that air provides...

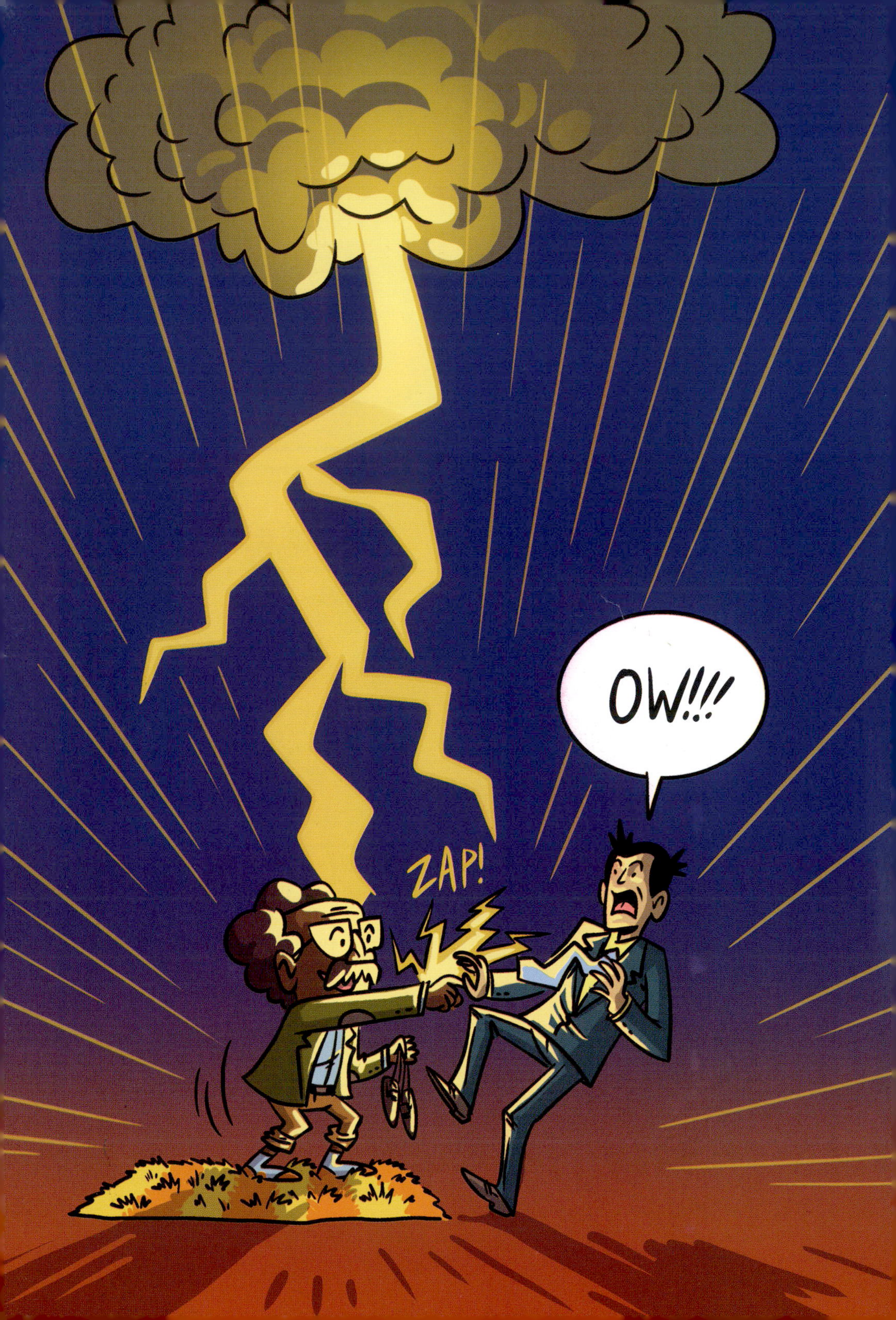
OW!!!
ZAP!

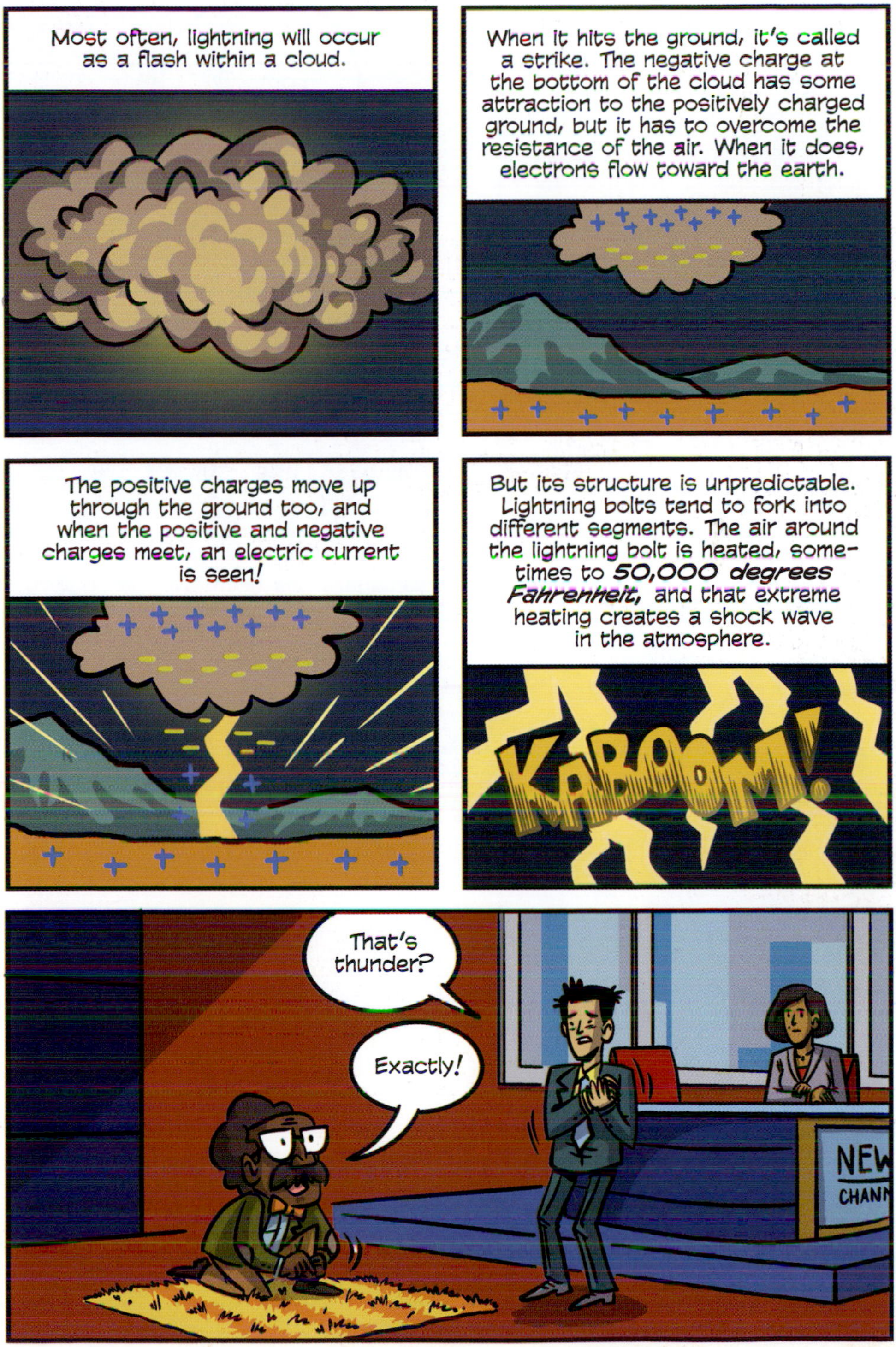
Most often, lightning will occur as a flash within a cloud.
When it hits the ground, it's called a strike. The negative charge at the bottom of the cloud has some attraction to the positively charged ground, but it has to overcome the resistance of the air. When it does, electrons flow toward the earth.
The positive charges move up through the ground too, and when the positive and negative charges meet, an electric current is seen!
But its structure is unpredictable. Lightning bolts tend to fork into different segments. The air around the lightning bolt is heated, sometimes to ***50,000 degrees Fahrenheit,*** and that extreme heating creates a shock wave in the atmosphere.
KABOOM!
That's thunder?
Exactly!
NEW
CHANN

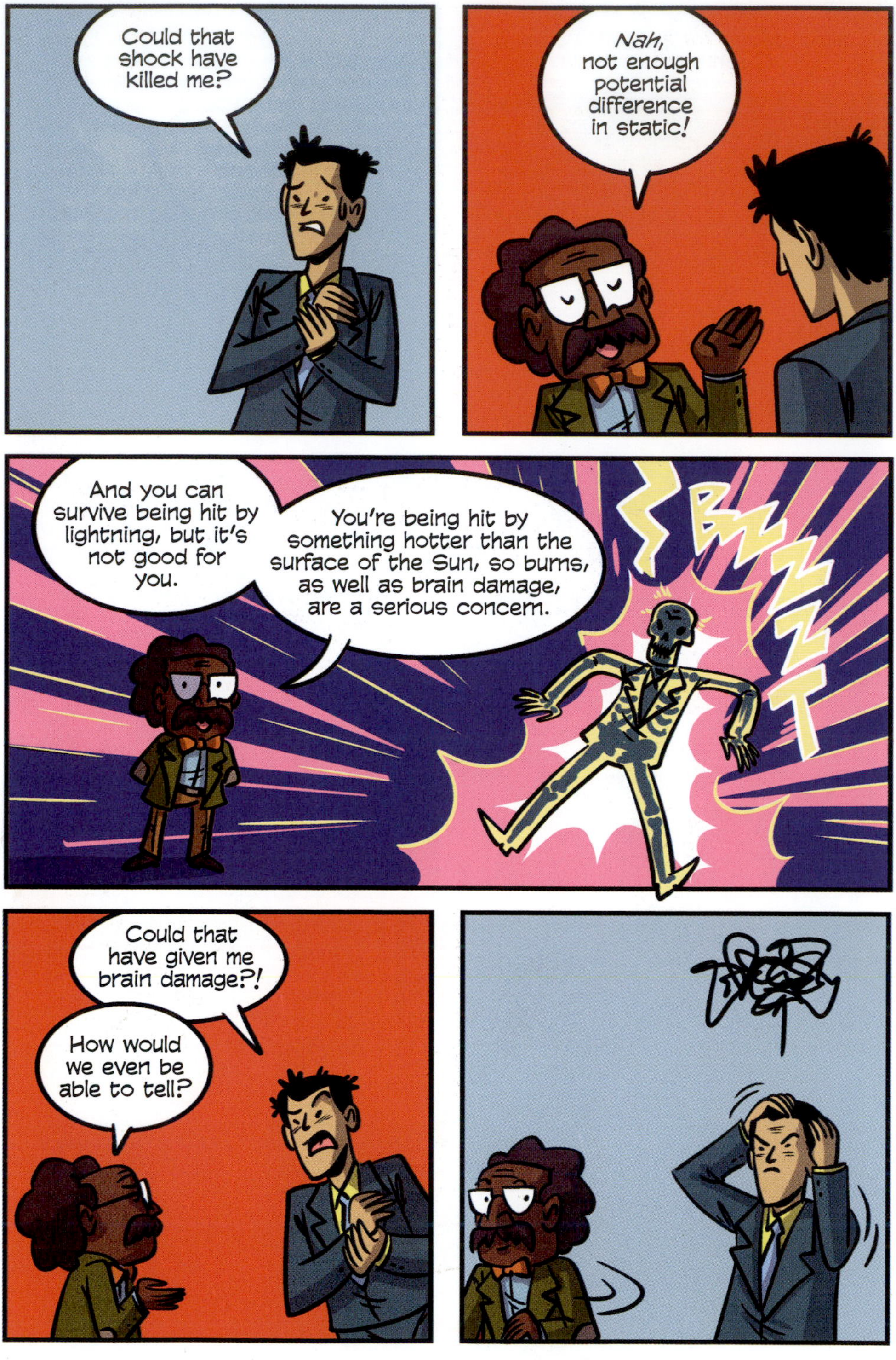
Could that shock have killed me?
Nah, not enough potential difference in static!
And you can survive being hit by lightning, but it's not good for you.
You're being hit by something hotter than the surface of the Sun, so burns, as well as brain damage, are a serious concern.
BZZZZT
Could that have given me brain damage?!
How would we even be able to tell?

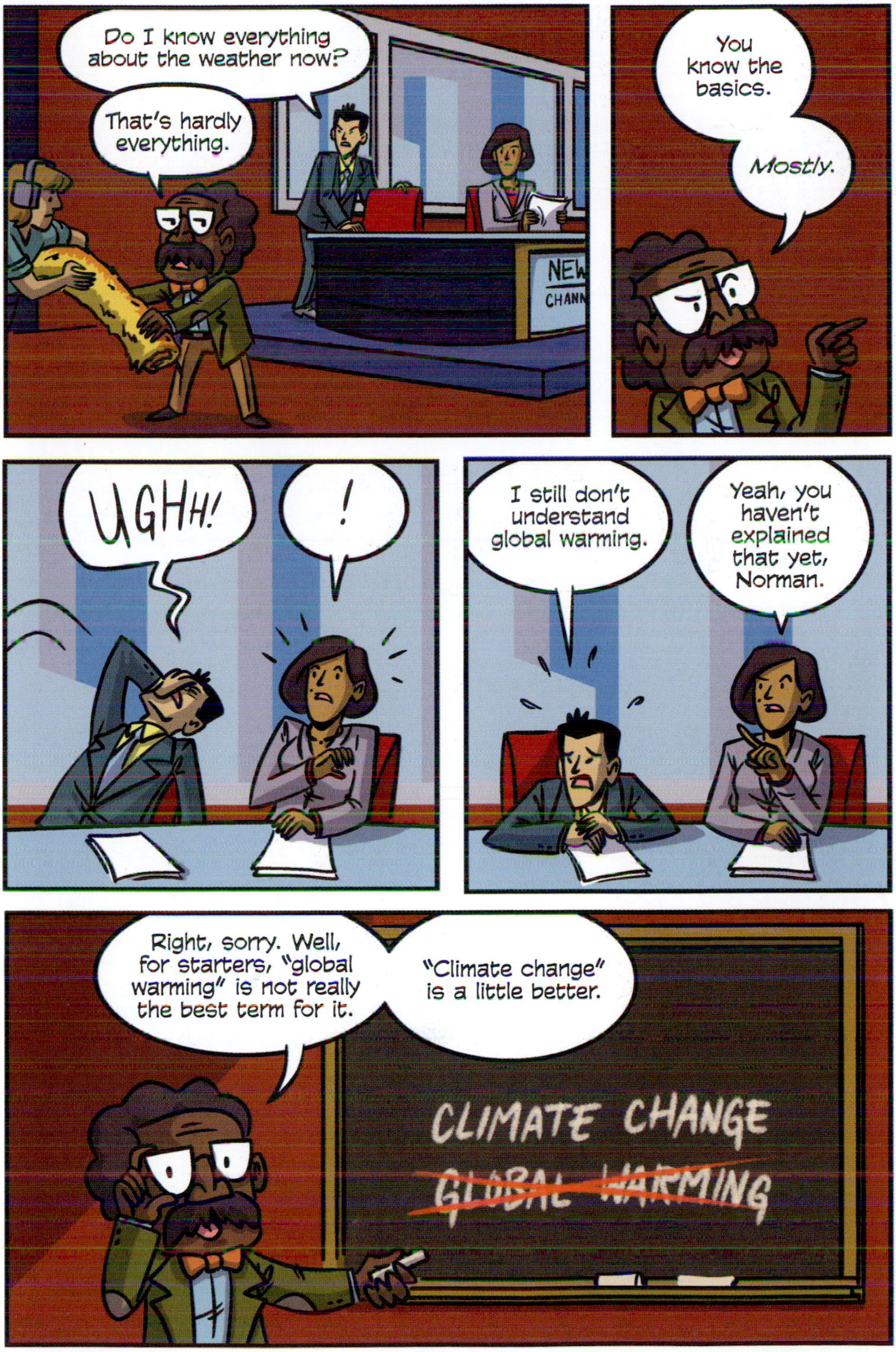
Do I know everything about the weather now?
That's hardly everything.
NEW
CHANN
You know the basics.
Mostly.
UGHH!
!
I still don't understand global warming.
Yeah, you haven't explained that yet, Norman.
Right, sorry. Well, for starters, "global warming" is not really the best term for it.
"Climate change" is a little better.
CLIMATE CHANGE
~~GLOBAL WARMING~~

Day to day, the temperature changes a lot naturally. But we've been keeping detailed daily records of the weather across the globe for about 150 years.

We average the temperatures for a day over the entire globe and compare it against the previous averages. Over time, those averages have gone up, especially in recent years, raising the average temperature steadily higher.

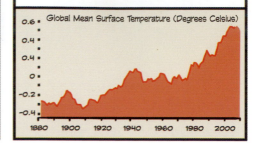

Global Mean Surface Temperature (Degrees Celsius)

Now, one hot day in winter doesn't always mean the end of the world, we know there are going to be variations. But several years of hotter-than-average temperatures, month after month, are a serious concern.

We know that human industries put chemicals into the atmosphere, which are trapping heat.

cough

We produce methane, which results from decomposition, such as garbage in a landfill. It's also a by-product of agriculture and livestock practices.

Carbon dioxide is a by-product of burning fossil fuels and of deforestation, so any time you drive or burn things for heat or fuel, it's created.

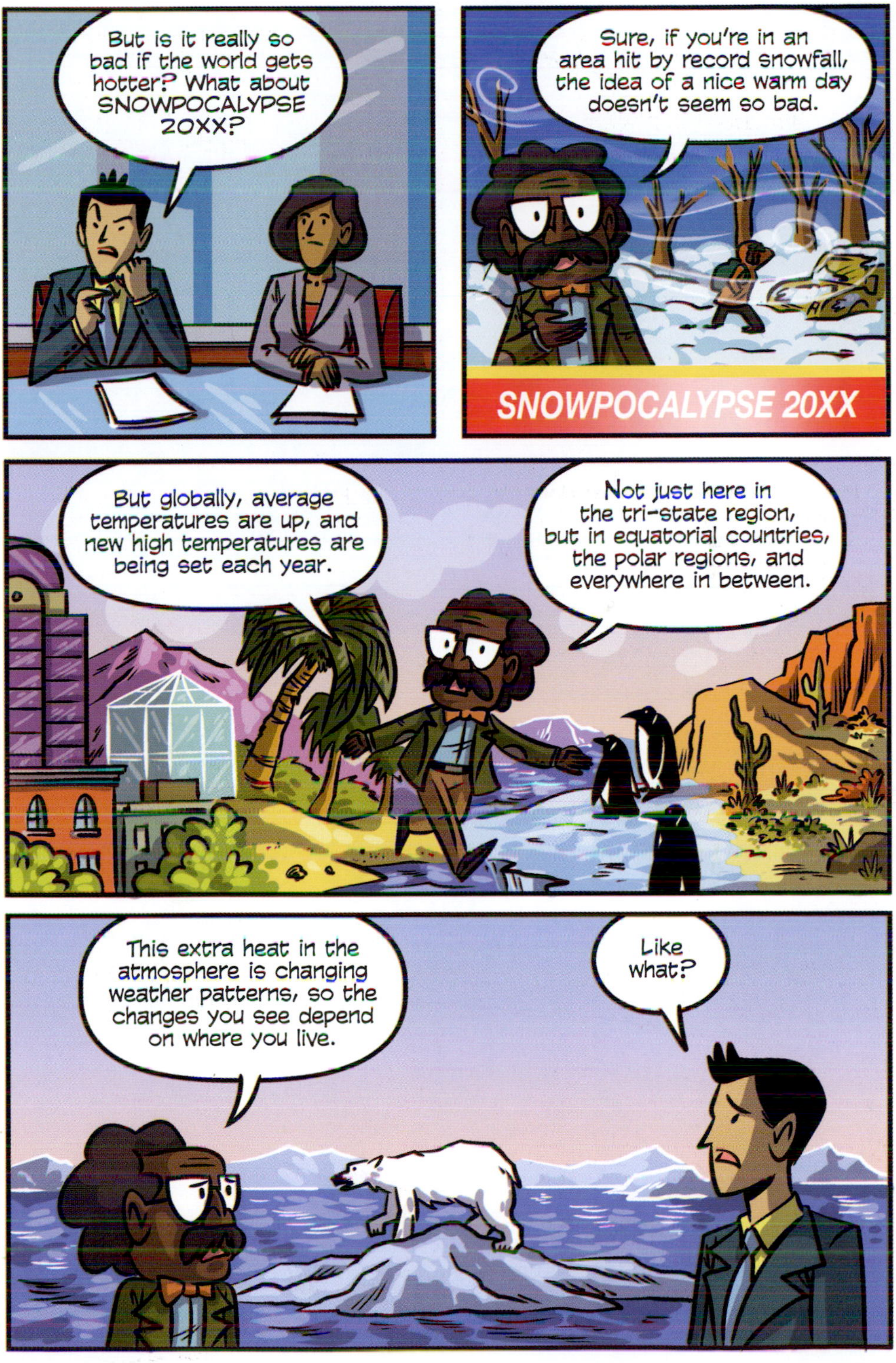
But is it really so bad if the world gets hotter? What about SNOWPOCALYPSE 20XX?
Sure, if you're in an area hit by record snowfall, the idea of a nice warm day doesn't seem so bad.
SNOWPOCALYPSE 20XX
But globally, average temperatures are up, and new high temperatures are being set each year.
Not just here in the tri-state region, but in equatorial countries, the polar regions, and everywhere in between.
This extra heat in the atmosphere is changing weather patterns, so the changes you see depend on where you live.
Like what?

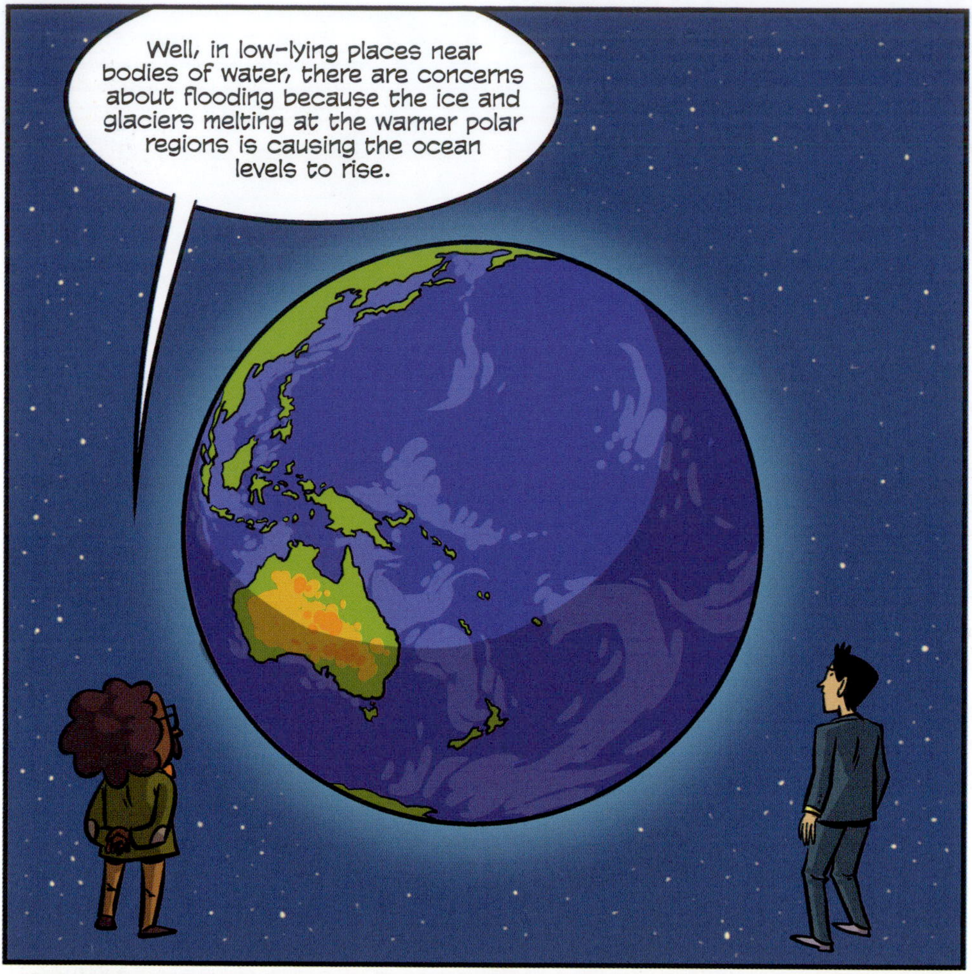
Well, in low-lying places near bodies of water, there are concerns about flooding because the ice and glaciers melting at the warmer polar regions is causing the ocean levels to rise.

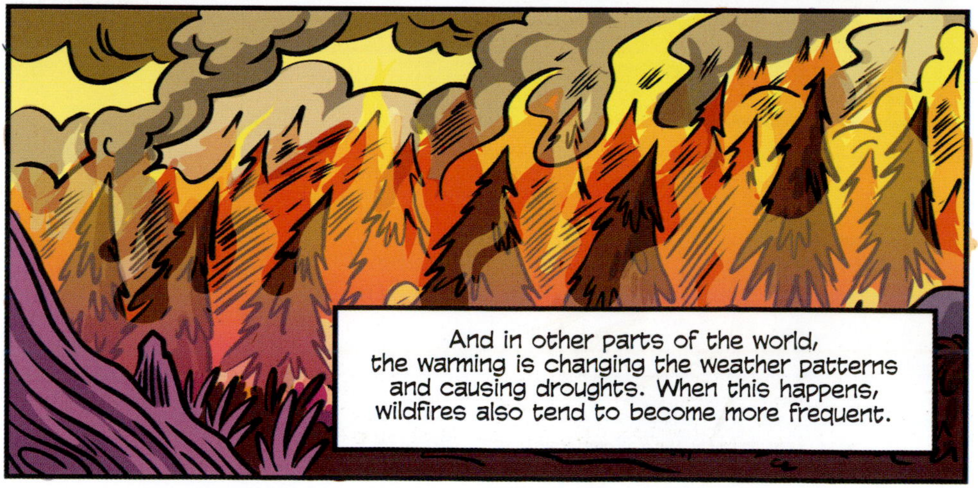
And in other parts of the world, the warming is changing the weather patterns and causing droughts. When this happens, wildfires also tend to become more frequent.

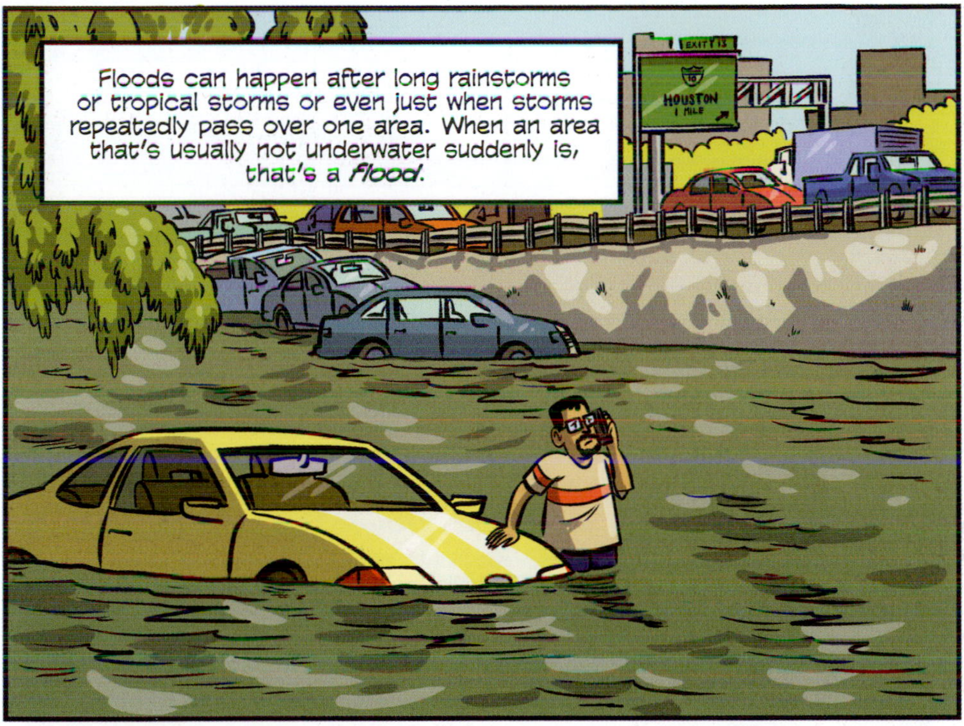
Floods can happen after long rainstorms or tropical storms or even just when storms repeatedly pass over one area. When an area that's usually not underwater suddenly is, that's a *flood*.
EXIT 13
10
HOUSTON
1 MILE

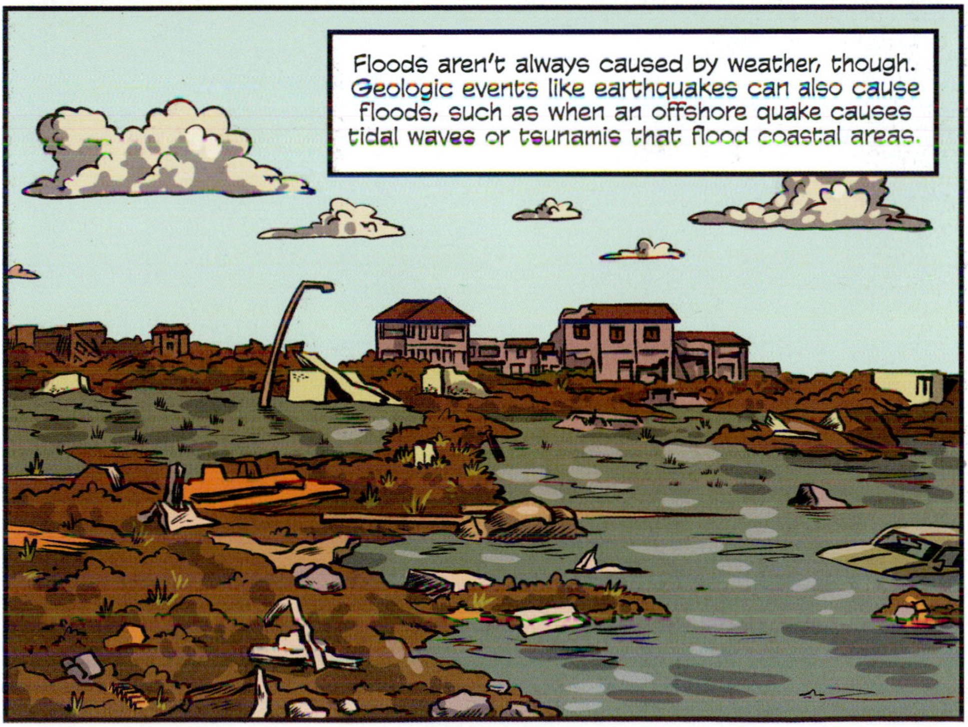
Floods aren't always caused by weather, though. Geologic events like earthquakes can also cause floods, such as when an offshore quake causes tidal waves or tsunamis that flood coastal areas.

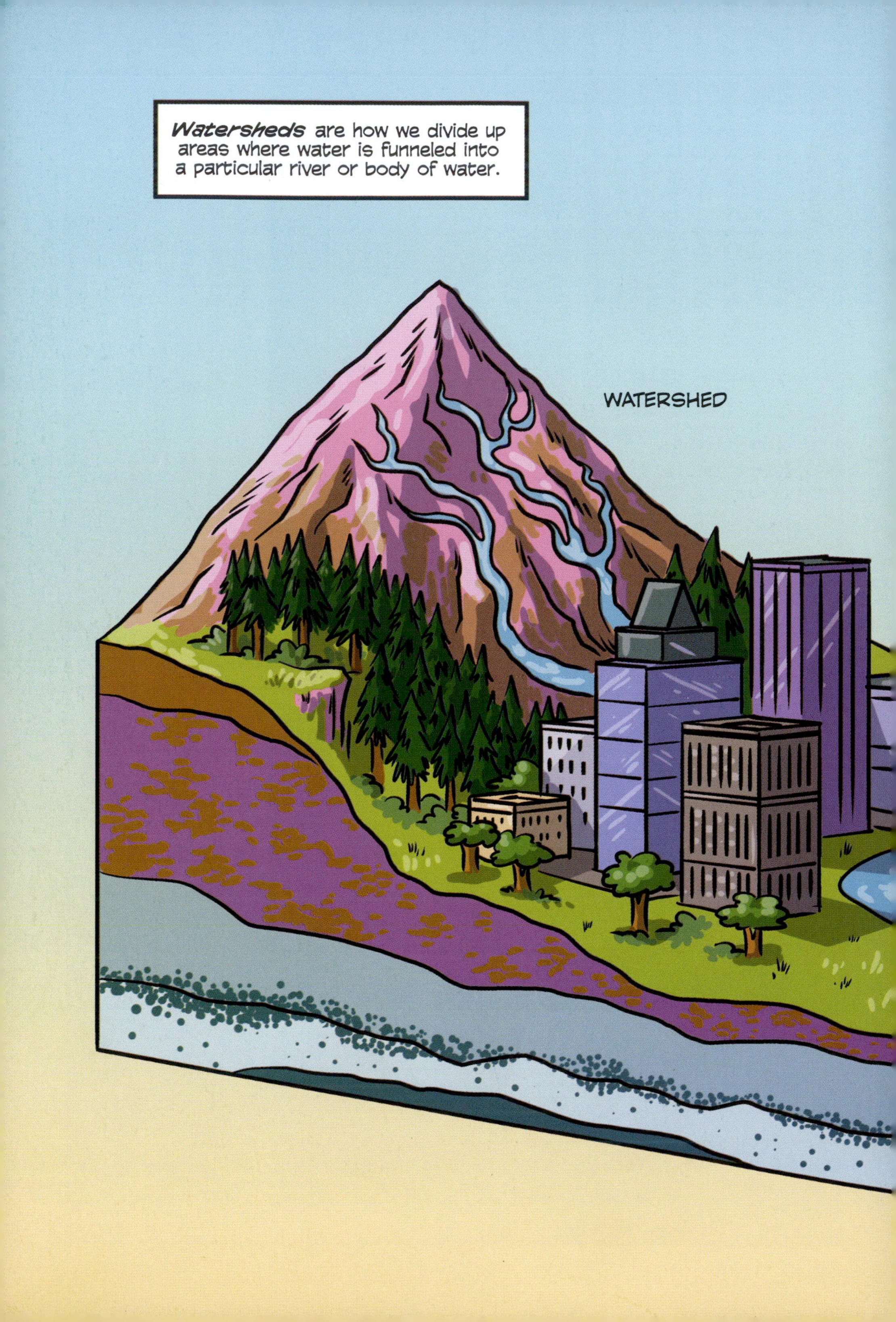
Watersheds are how we divide up areas where water is funneled into a particular river or body of water.
WATERSHED

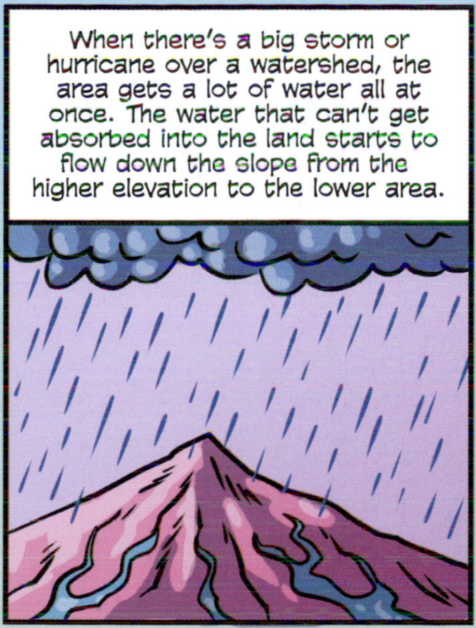
When there's a big storm or hurricane over a watershed, the area gets a lot of water all at once. The water that can't get absorbed into the land starts to flow down the slope from the higher elevation to the lower area.

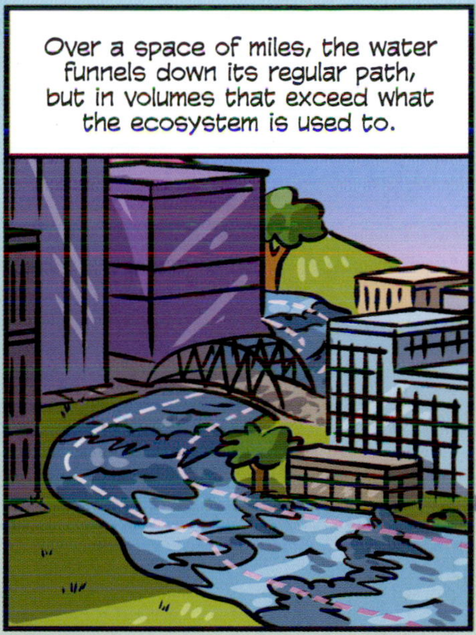
Over a space of miles, the water funnels down its regular path, but in volumes that exceed what the ecosystem is used to.

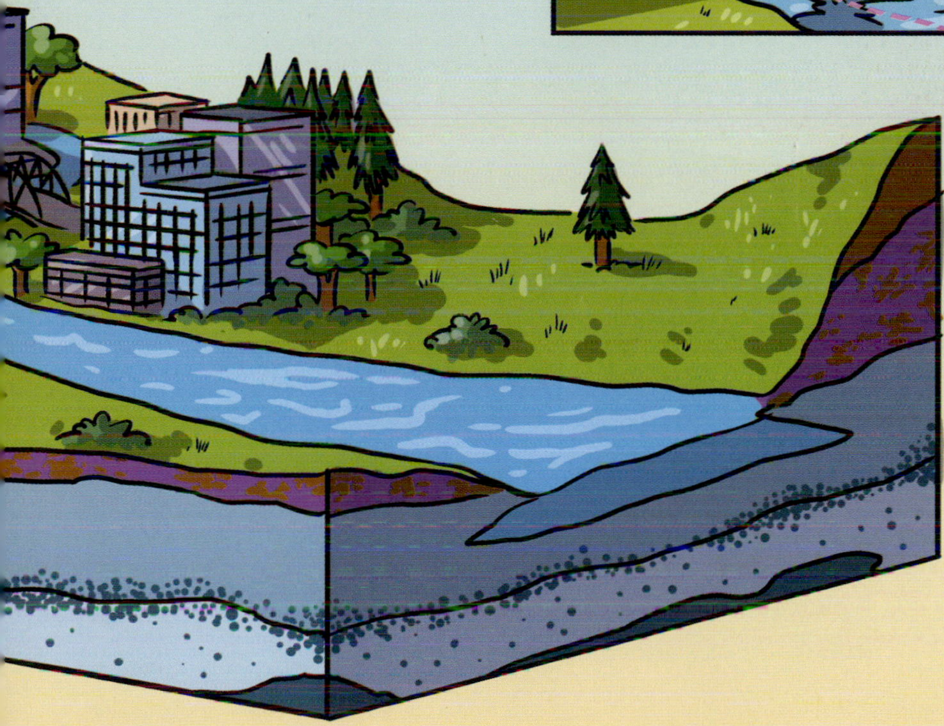

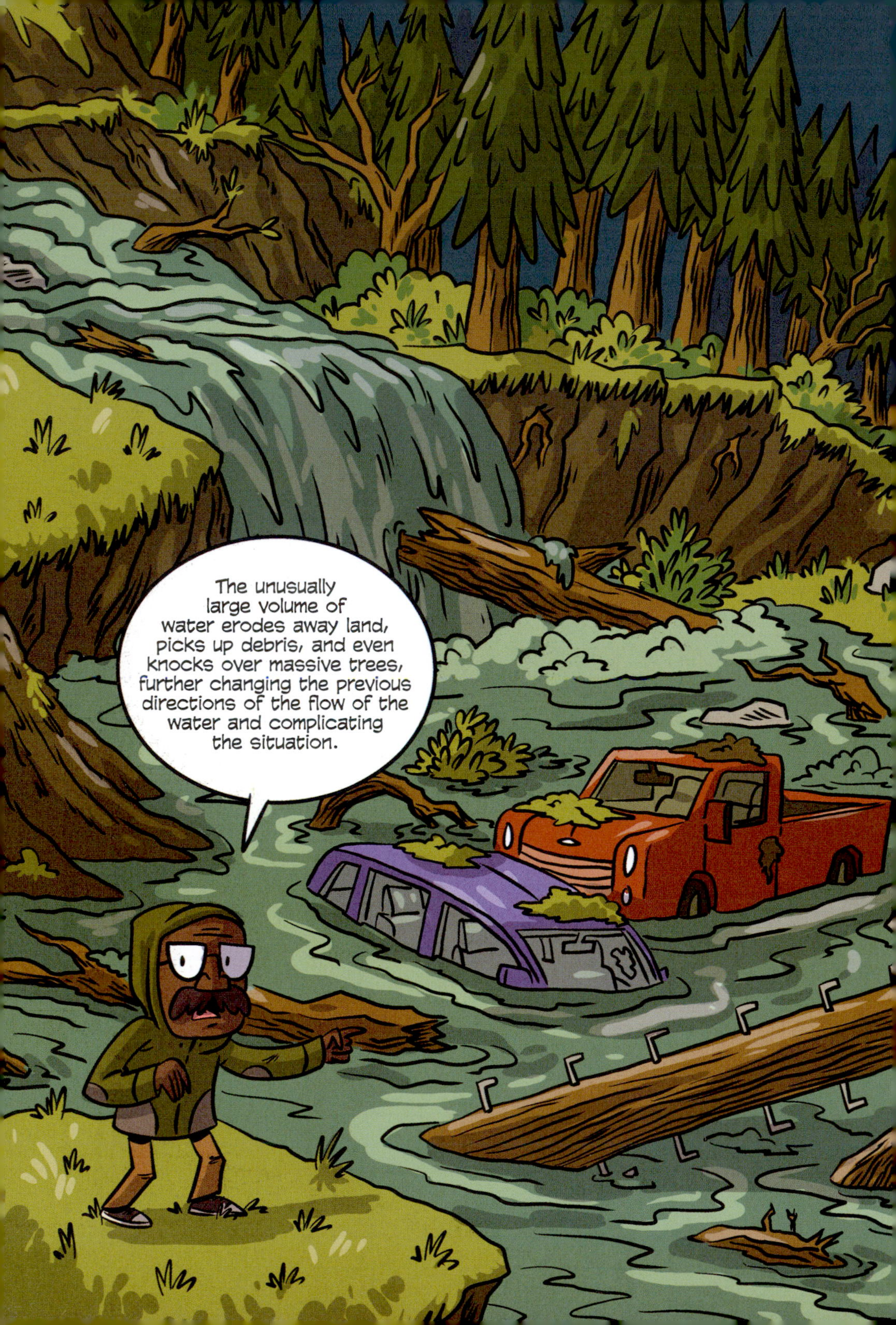
The unusually large volume of water erodes away land, picks up debris, and even knocks over massive trees, further changing the previous directions of the flow of the water and complicating the situation.

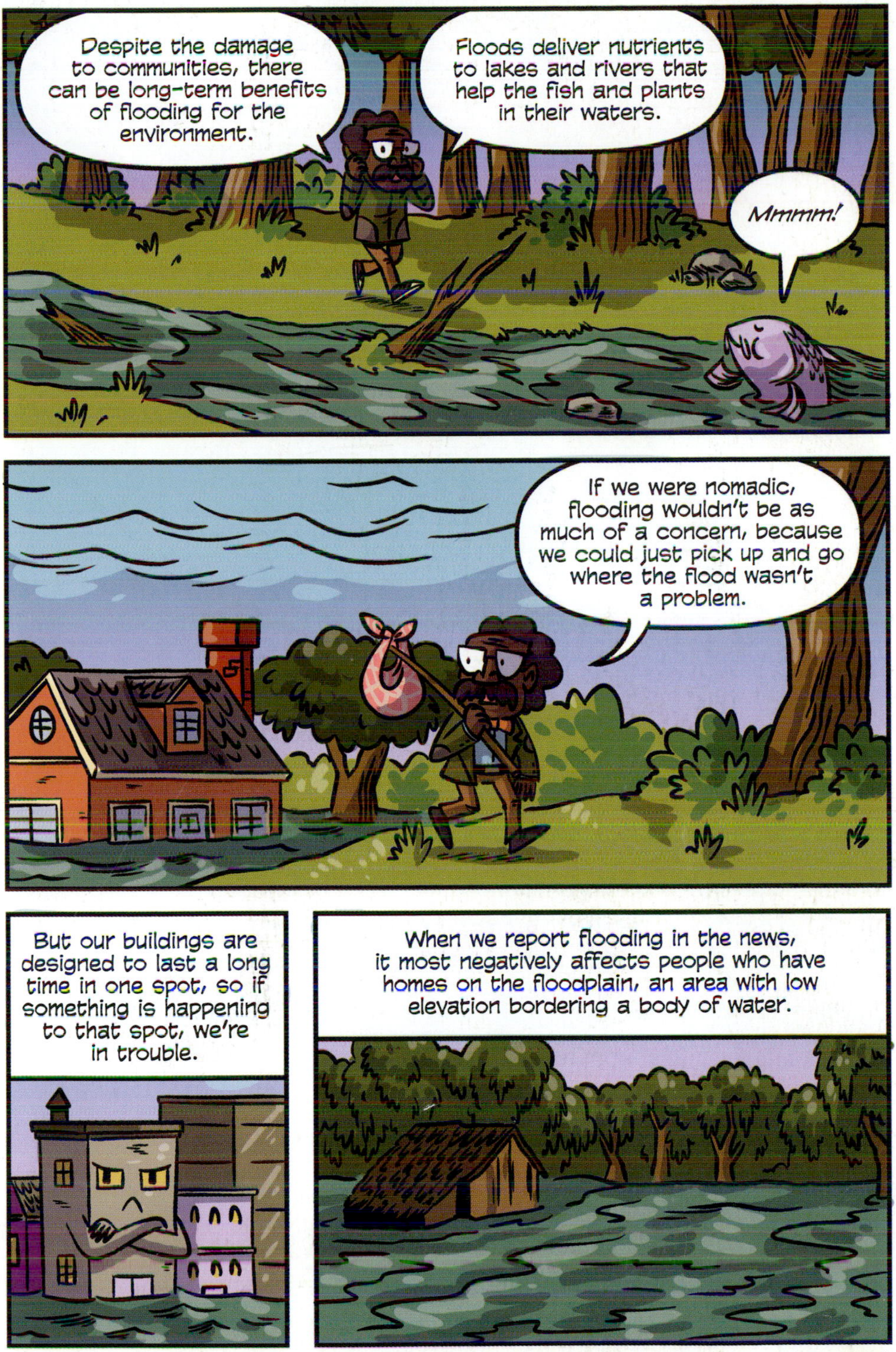
Despite the damage to communities, there can be long-term benefits of flooding for the environment.
Floods deliver nutrients to lakes and rivers that help the fish and plants in their waters.
Mmmm!
If we were nomadic, flooding wouldn't be as much of a concern, because we could just pick up and go where the flood wasn't a problem.
But our buildings are designed to last a long time in one spot, so if something is happening to that spot, we're in trouble.
When we report flooding in the news, it most negatively affects people who have homes on the floodplain, an area with low elevation bordering a body of water.

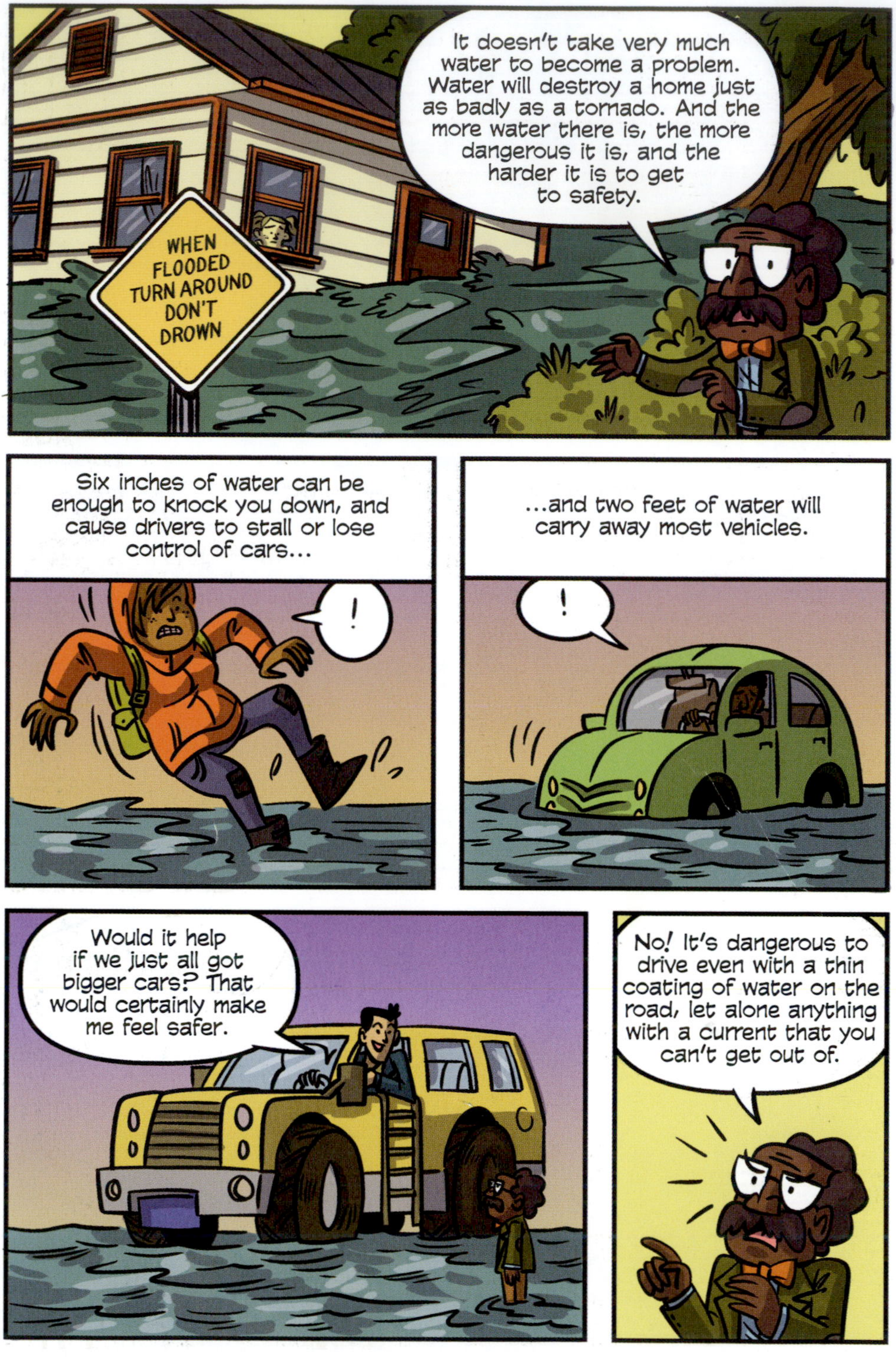

It doesn't take very much water to become a problem. Water will destroy a home just as badly as a tornado. And the more water there is, the more dangerous it is, and the harder it is to get to safety.
WHEN FLOODED TURN AROUND DON'T DROWN
Six inches of water can be enough to knock you down, and cause drivers to stall or lose control of cars...
!
...and two feet of water will carry away most vehicles.
!
Would it help if we just all got bigger cars? That would certainly make me feel safer.
No! It's dangerous to drive even with a thin coating of water on the road, let alone anything with a current that you can't get out of.

A continued rainfall of one inch of rain per hour is enough to start causing problems in urban areas with impenetrable surfaces, which means buildings, roads, and sidewalks. Water sits on the surface and collects there instead of going into the dirt, so there's more danger of flooding in cities.

It can even stop raining, but there still be risk of flooding because of the volume of water making its way down the watershed.

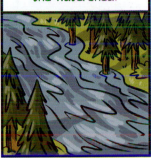

When Snowpocalypse 20XX eventualy begins to melt, one side effect may be that ice and snow are blocking the city's drains, and some flooding could result if they aren't cleared in time.

And that's just in urban parts—there's also a lot of damage done to crops.

But plants need water to live! Floods should be great for them!

Chase, remember when I told you that you didn't need to water your cactus every day? And you kept doing it and then the cactus turned black?

No.

Plants need water, but too much can cause mold or mildew to appear, or it can make the plant sick.

Right, Connie!

Plus, when the soil is waterlogged, the root system isn't supported in the softer mud, and the weight of the plant can pull the whole thing down.

You'll often see trees fall after a storm, which adds to another concern after flooding or after a long period of rain—mudslides!

CRASH!

Mudslides usually happen after weeks or months of water seeping into the ground, like after a period of heavy rainfall or when snow melts.

Sometimes the water even seeps into hard rock layers and breaks it apart.

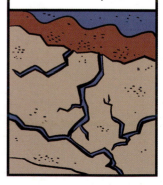

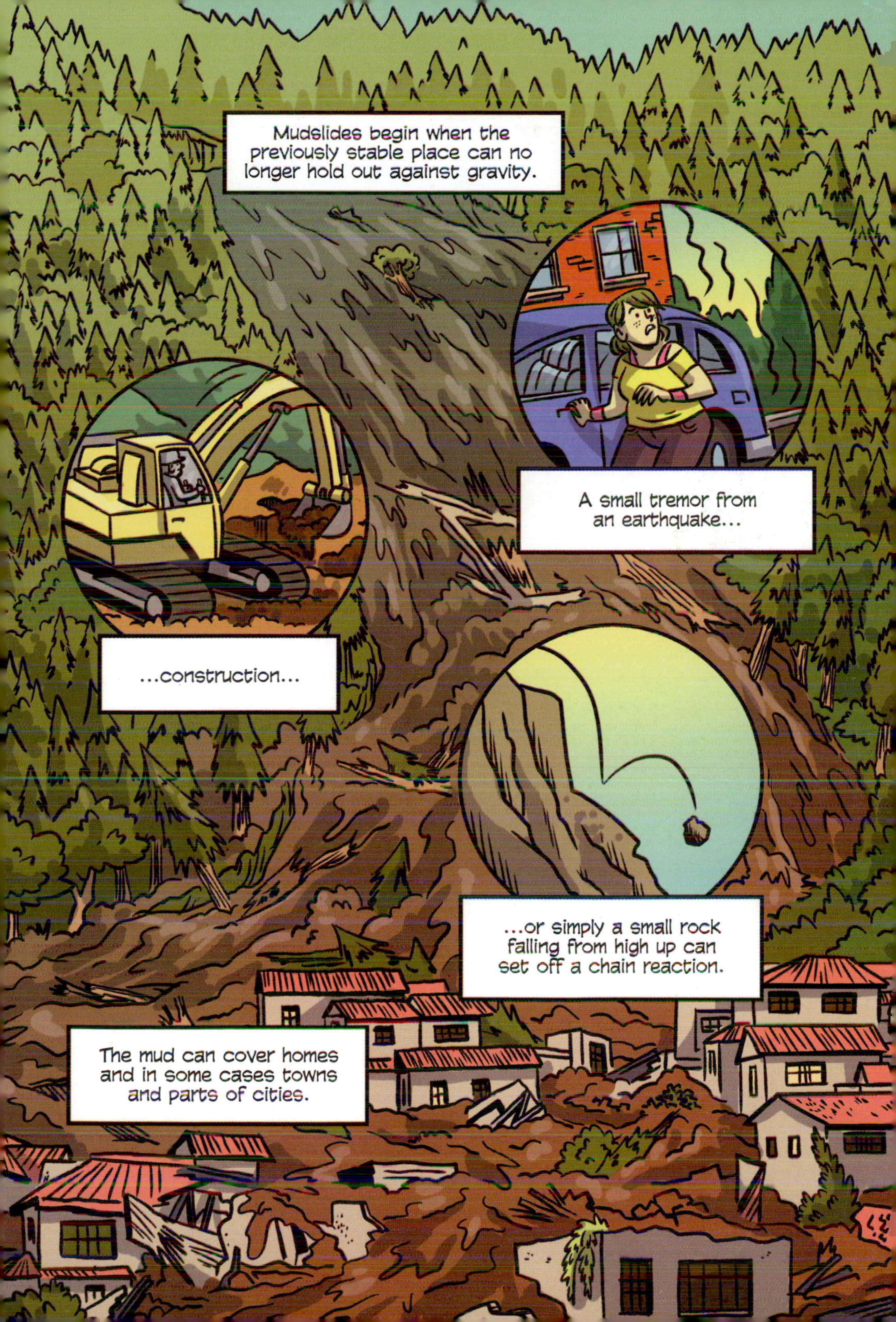
Mudslides begin when the previously stable place can no longer hold out against gravity.
A small tremor from an earthquake...
...construction...
...or simply a small rock falling from high up can set off a chain reaction.
The mud can cover homes and in some cases towns and parts of cities.

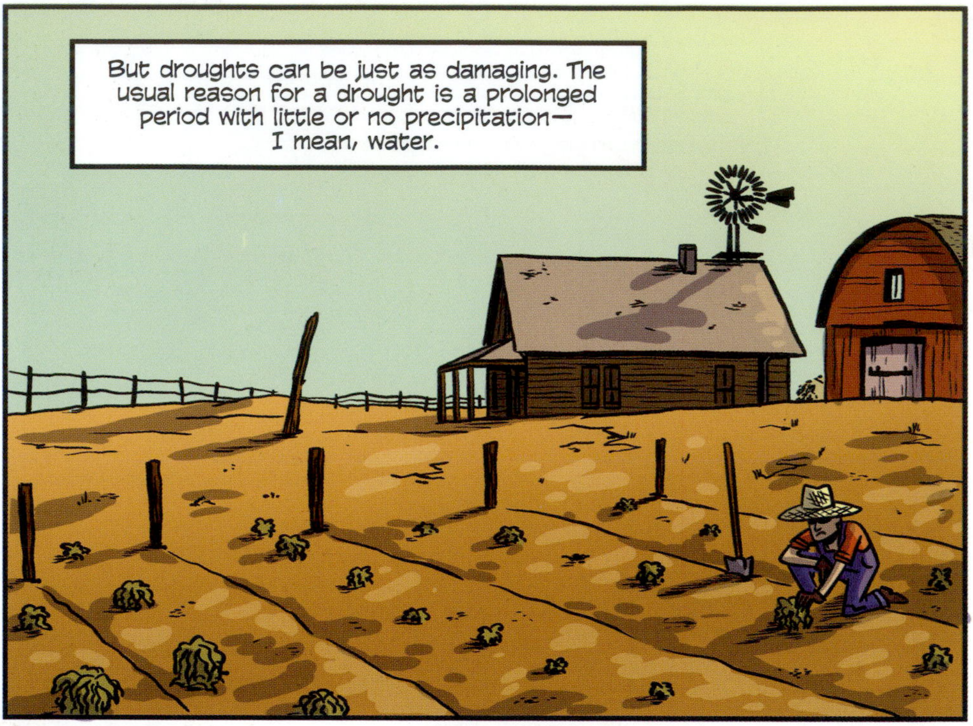
But droughts can be just as damaging. The usual reason for a drought is a prolonged period with little or no precipitation—I mean, water.

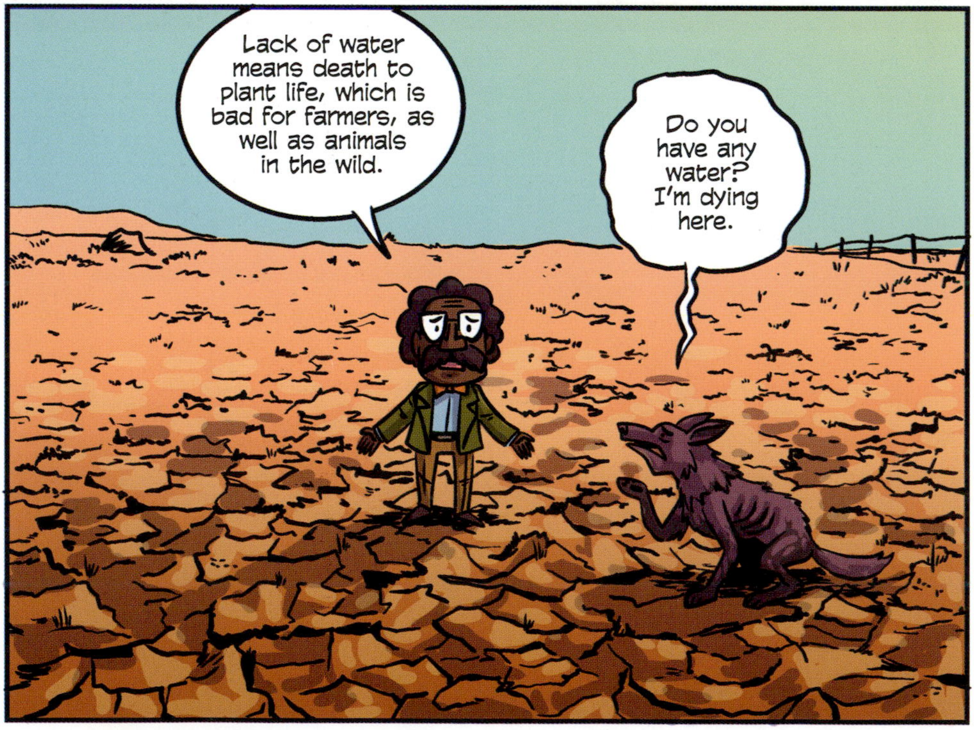
Lack of water means death to plant life, which is bad for farmers, as well as animals in the wild.
Do you have any water? I'm dying here.

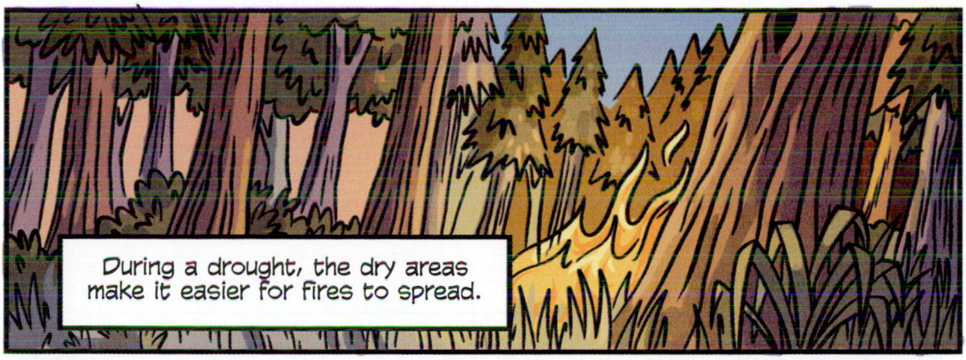
During a drought, the dry areas make it easier for fires to spread.

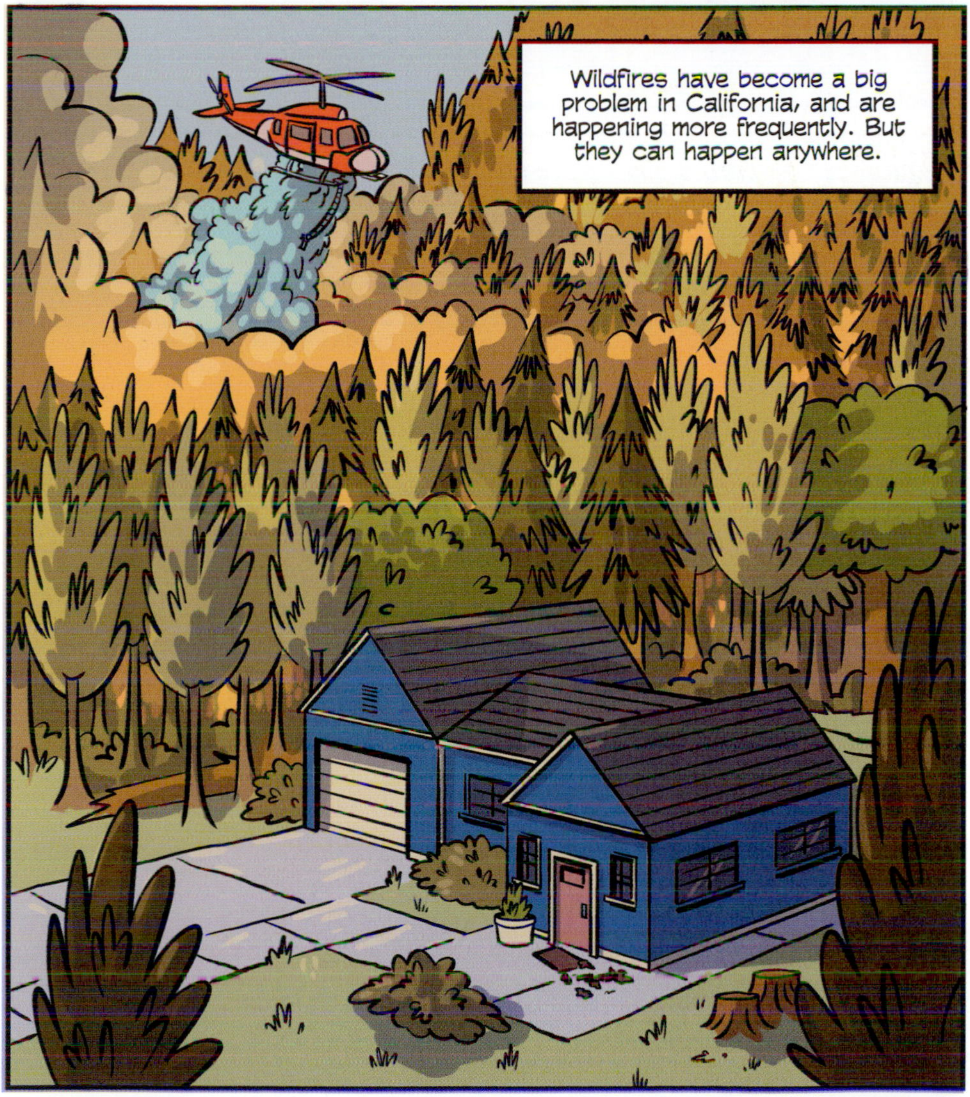
Wildfires have become a big problem in California, and are happening more frequently. But they can happen anywhere.

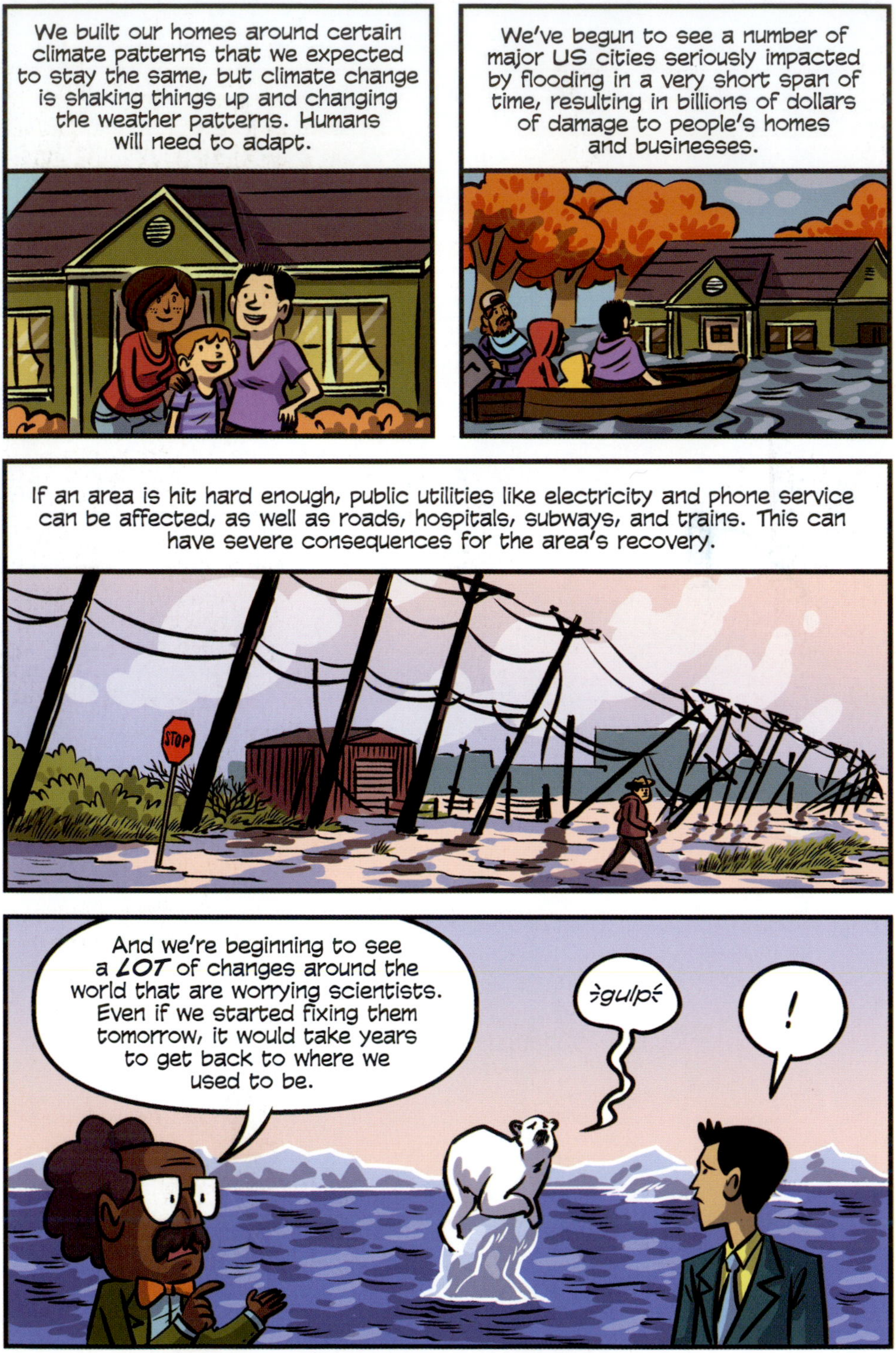
We built our homes around certain climate patterns that we expected to stay the same, but climate change is shaking things up and changing the weather patterns. Humans will need to adapt.
We've begun to see a number of major US cities seriously impacted by flooding in a very short span of time, resulting in billions of dollars of damage to people's homes and businesses.
If an area is hit hard enough, public utilities like electricity and phone service can be affected, as well as roads, hospitals, subways, and trains. This can have severe consequences for the area's recovery.
STOP
And we're beginning to see a *LOT* of changes around the world that are worrying scientists. Even if we started fixing them tomorrow, it would take years to get back to where we used to be.
gulp
!

Norman, should I have been celebrating Earth Day all this time?

Would it help if I started now? Should I throw out my car and get an electric car? I'm a celebrity—I have the money to do that!

The *planet* Earth is going to be just fine!

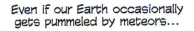

Even if our Earth occasionally gets pummeled by meteors...

...the Earth has been through dramatic climate change before... It's a survivor.

...Earth is going to keep on spinning around the Sun for an immeasurably long time.

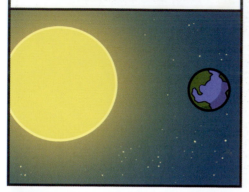

...At least up until the Sun turns into a red giant star!

Err...but there's nothing anyone can do to prevent that!

Phew!

NEWS
CHANNEL **6**

But you *should* do what you can to conserve power, use less fuel, and leave less of a carbon footprint.

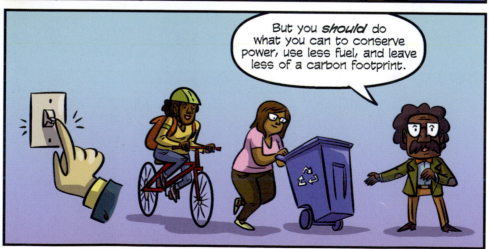

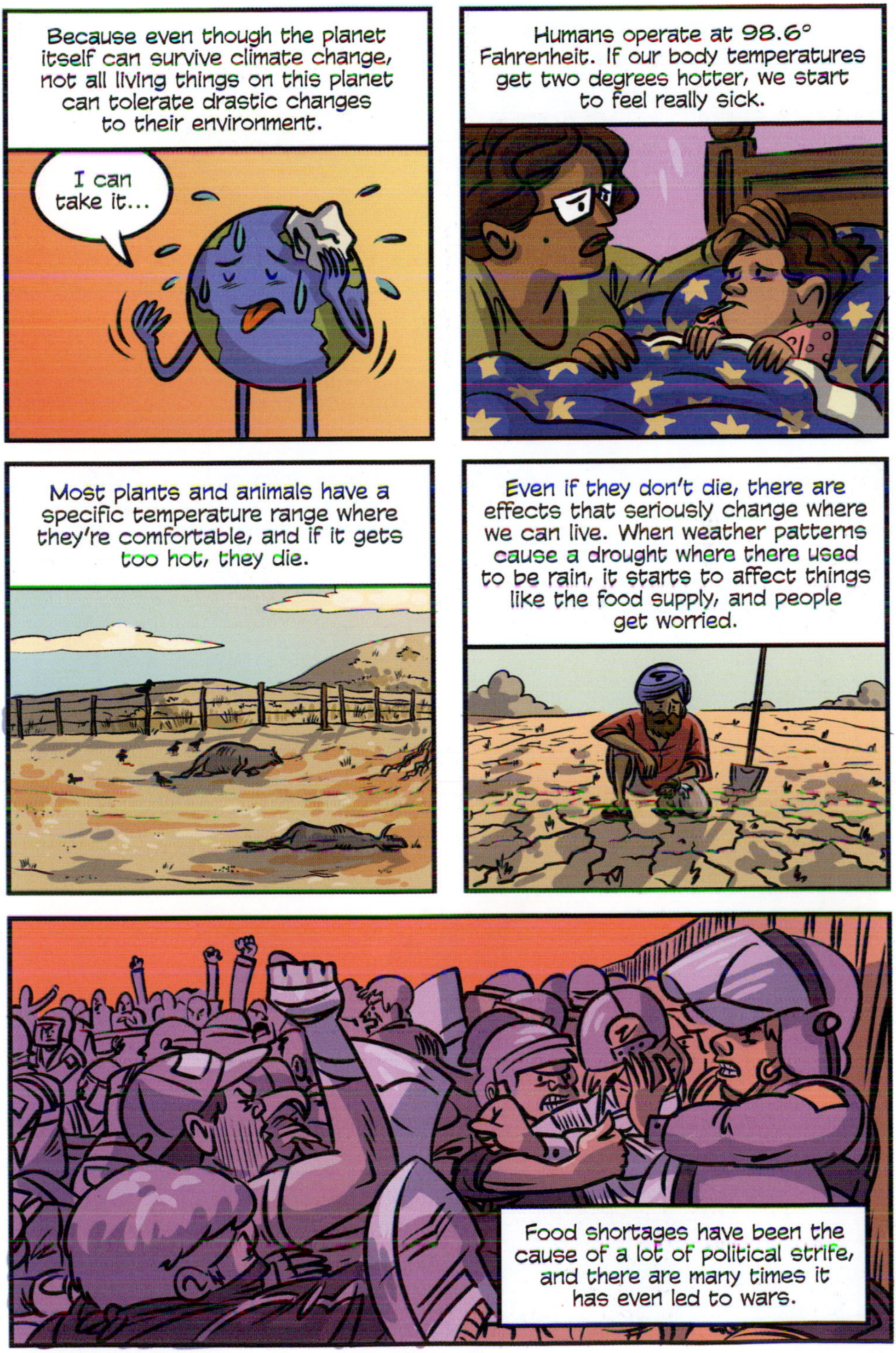
Because even though the planet itself can survive climate change, not all living things on this planet can tolerate drastic changes to their environment.
I can take it...
Humans operate at 98.6° Fahrenheit. If our body temperatures get two degrees hotter, we start to feel really sick.
Most plants and animals have a specific temperature range where they're comfortable, and if it gets too hot, they die.
Even if they don't die, there are effects that seriously change where we can live. When weather patterns cause a drought where there used to be rain, it starts to affect things like the food supply, and people get worried.
Food shortages have been the cause of a lot of political strife, and there are many times it has even led to wars.

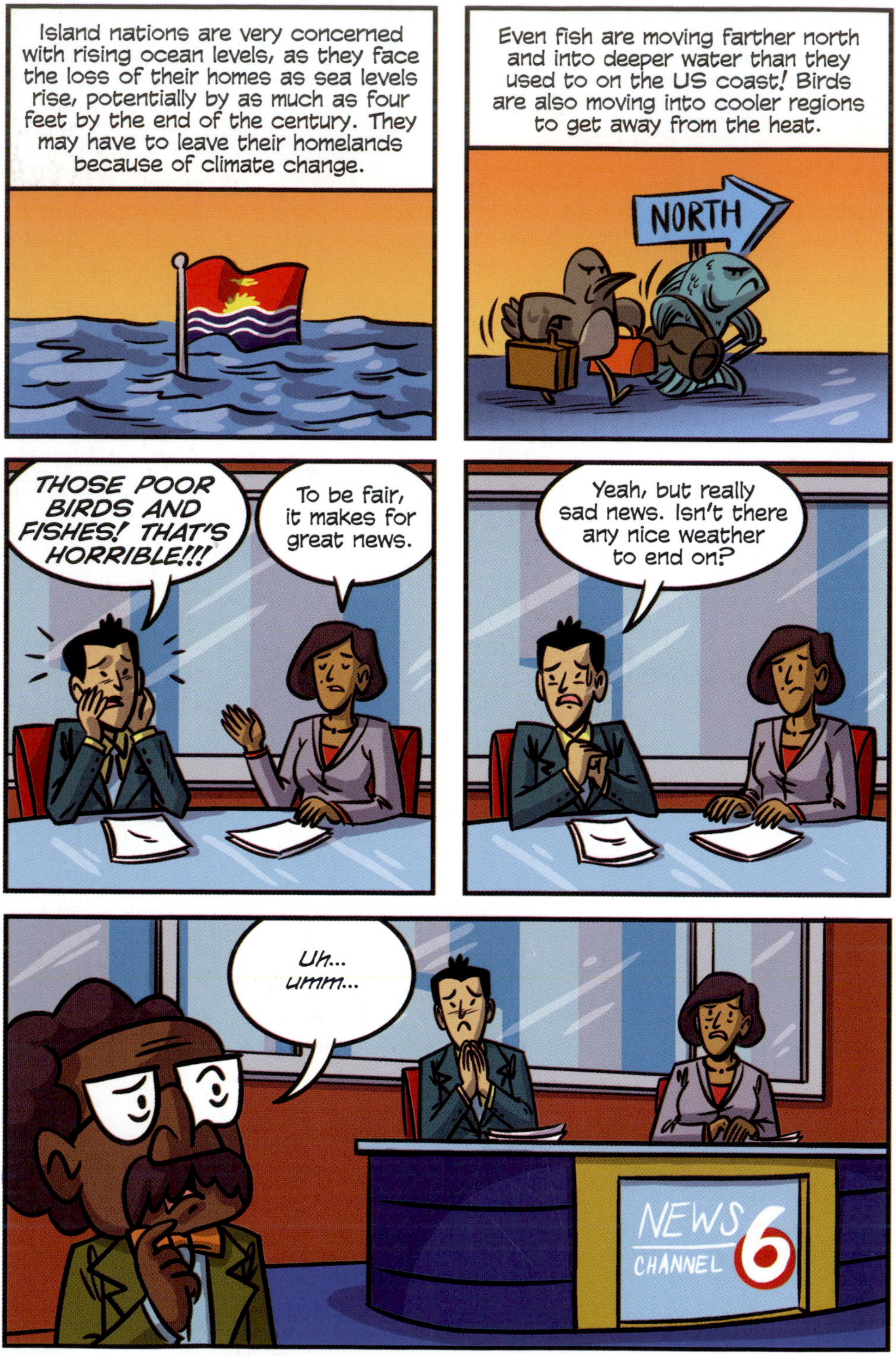
Island nations are very concerned with rising ocean levels, as they face the loss of their homes as sea levels rise, potentially by as much as four feet by the end of the century. They may have to leave their homelands because of climate change.
Even fish are moving farther north and into deeper water than they used to on the US coast! Birds are also moving into cooler regions to get away from the heat.
NORTH
THOSE POOR BIRDS AND FISHES! THAT'S HORRIBLE!!!
To be fair, it makes for great news.
Yeah, but really sad news. Isn't there any nice weather to end on?
Uh... umm...
NEWS CHANNEL 6

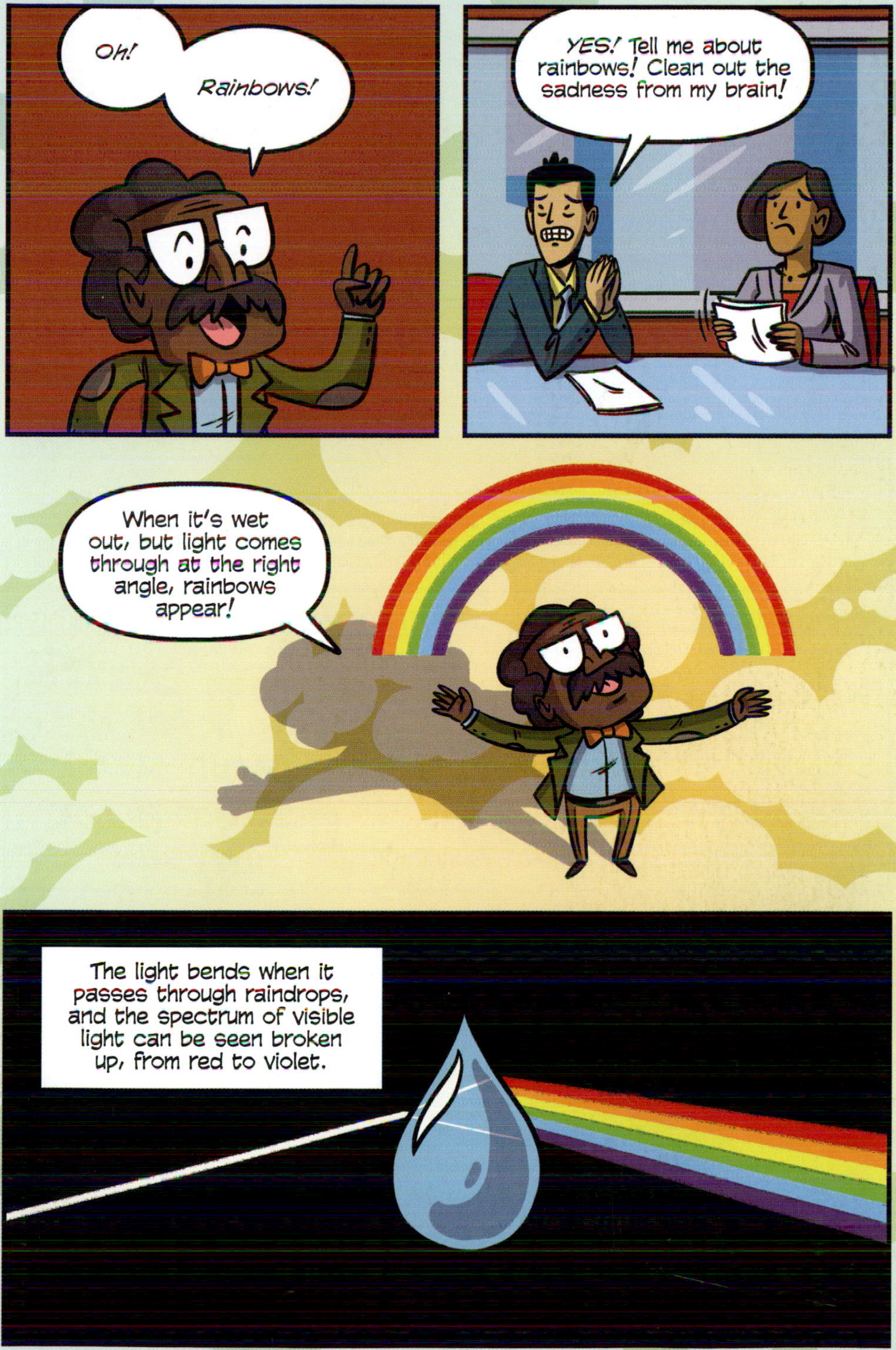
Oh!
Rainbows!
YES! Tell me about rainbows! Clean out the sadness from my brain!
When it's wet out, but light comes through at the right angle, rainbows appear!
The light bends when it passes through raindrops, and the spectrum of visible light can be seen broken up, from red to violet.

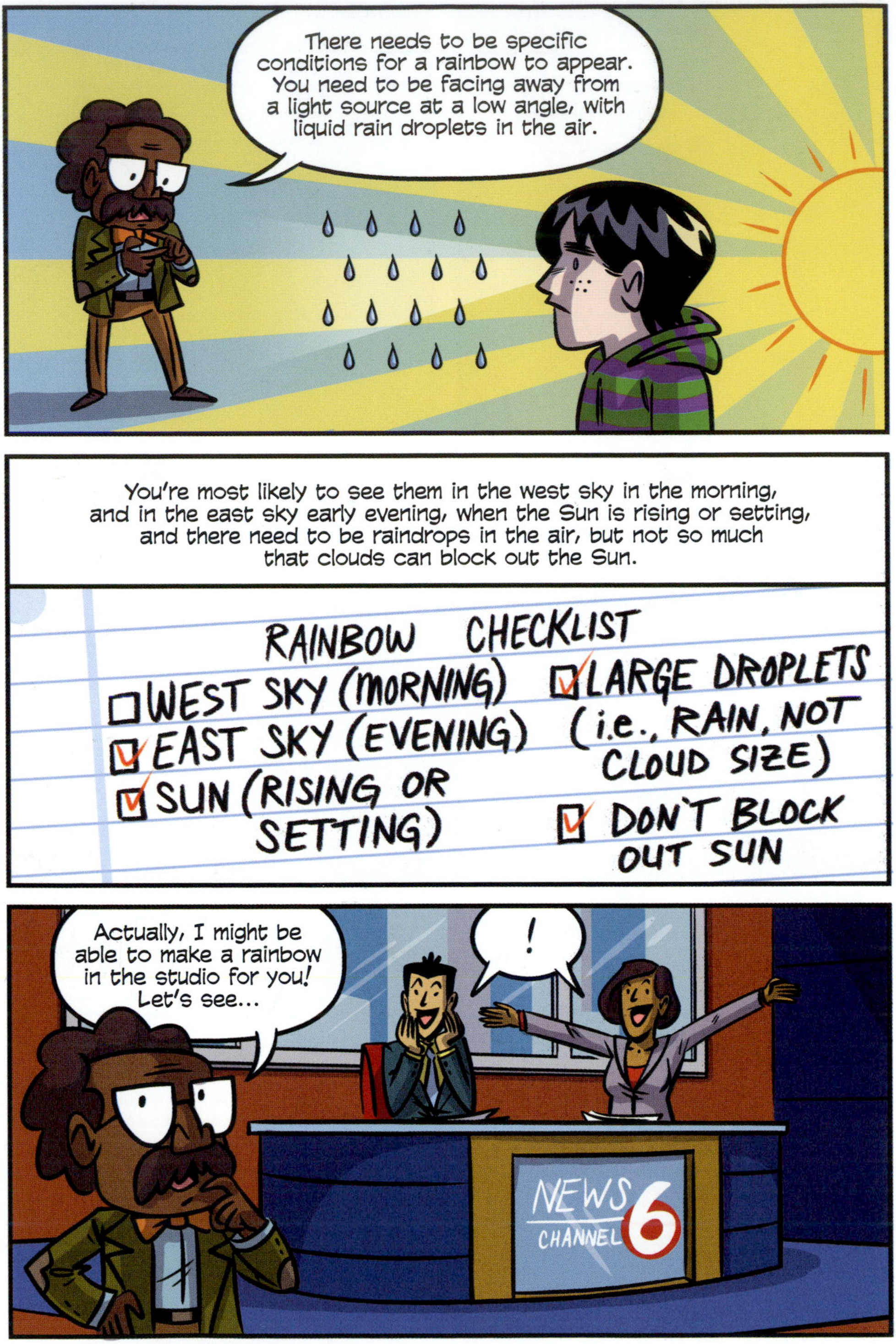
There needs to be specific conditions for a rainbow to appear. You need to be facing away from a light source at a low angle, with liquid rain droplets in the air.
You're most likely to see them in the west sky in the morning, and in the east sky early evening, when the Sun is rising or setting, and there need to be raindrops in the air, but not so much that clouds can block out the Sun.
RAINBOW CHECKLIST
WEST SKY (MORNING)
EAST SKY (EVENING)
SUN (RISING OR SETTING)
LARGE DROPLETS (i.e., RAIN, NOT CLOUD SIZE)
DON'T BLOCK OUT SUN
Actually, I might be able to make a rainbow in the studio for you! Let's see...
!
NEWS CHANNEL 6

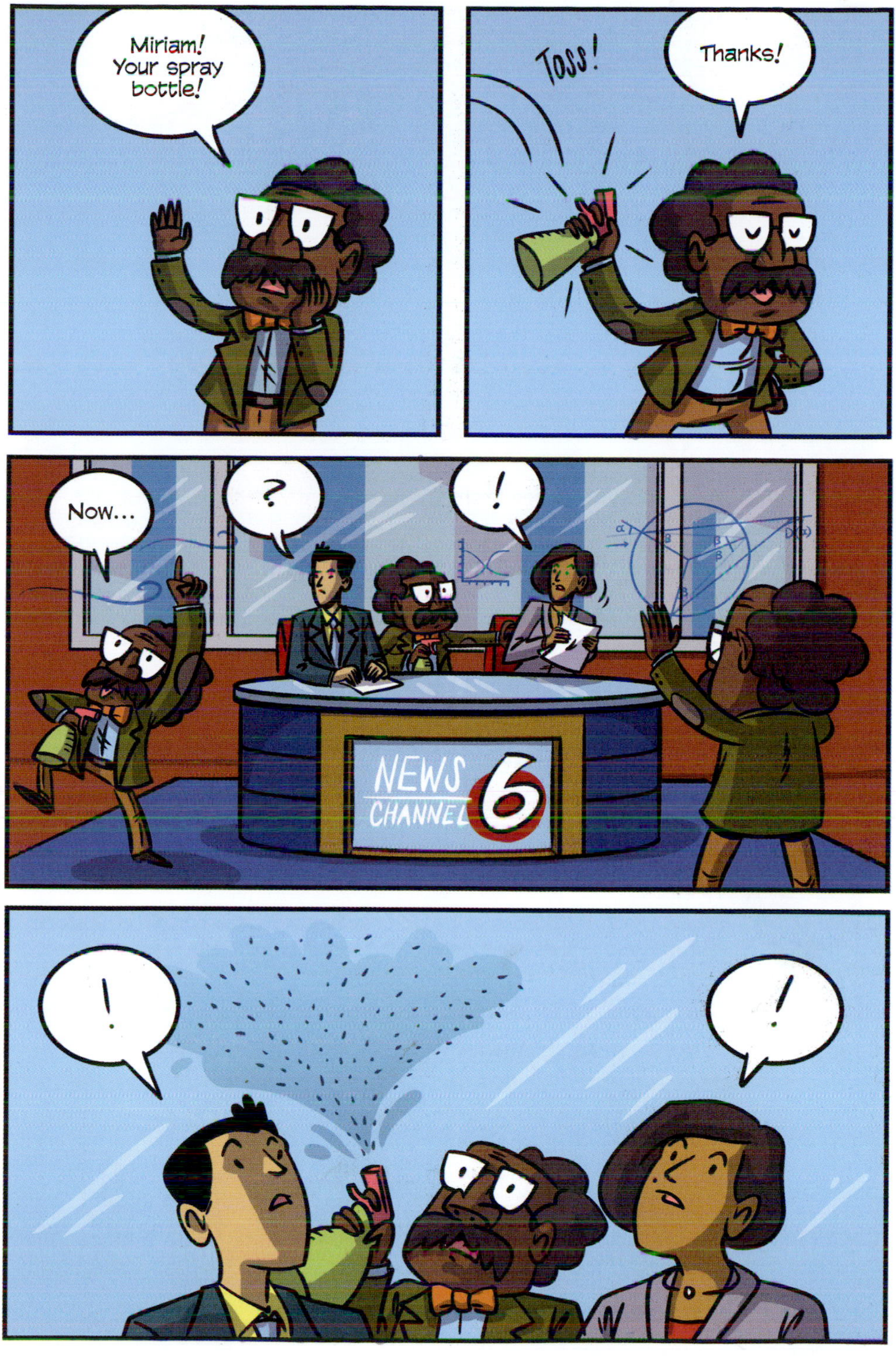
Miriam! Your spray bottle!
TOSS!
Thanks!
Now...
?
!
NEWS CHANNEL 6
!
!

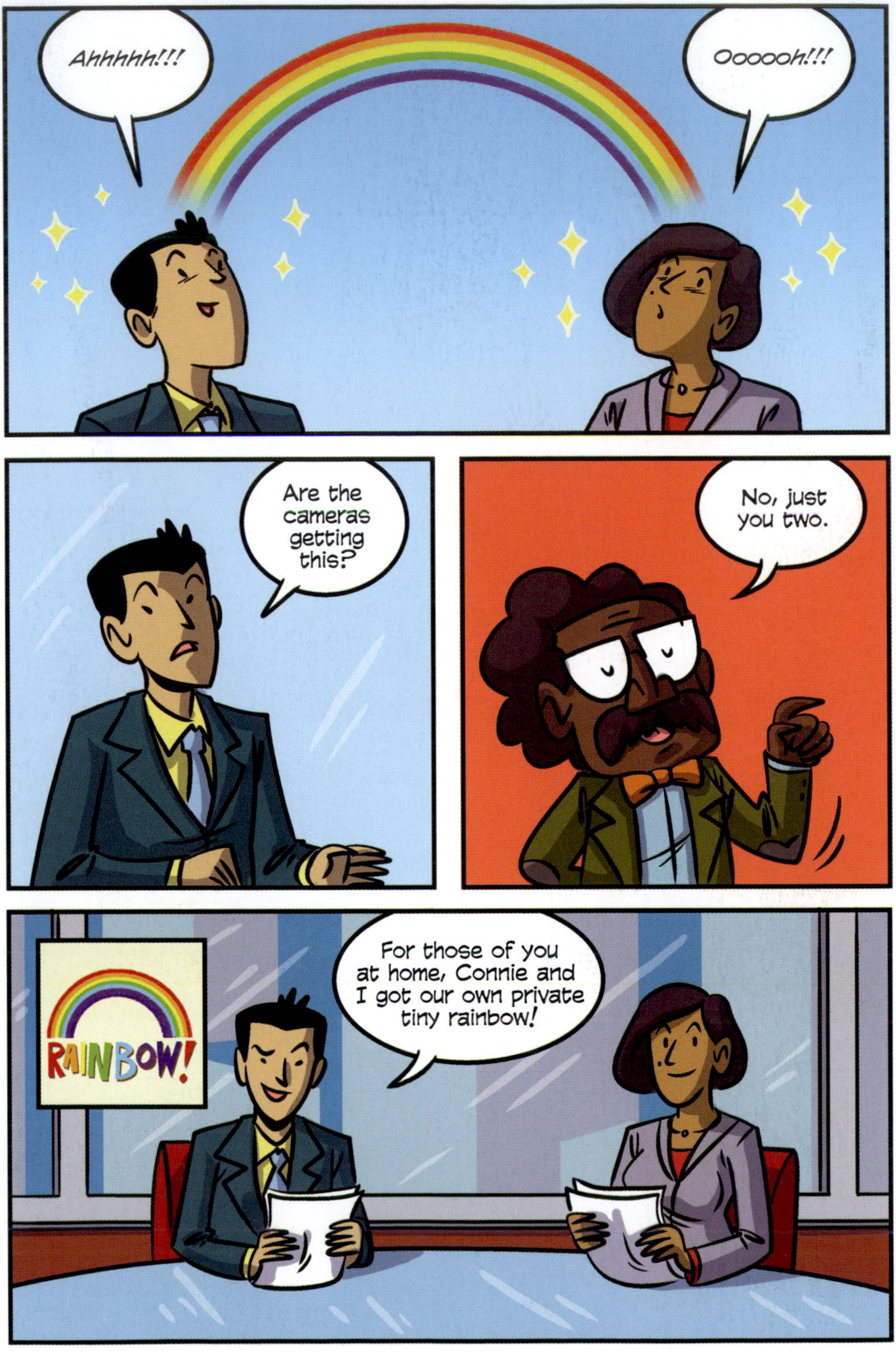
Ahhhhh!!!
Oooooh!!!
Are the cameras getting this?
No, just you two.
RAINBOW!
For those of you at home, Connie and I got our own private tiny rainbow!

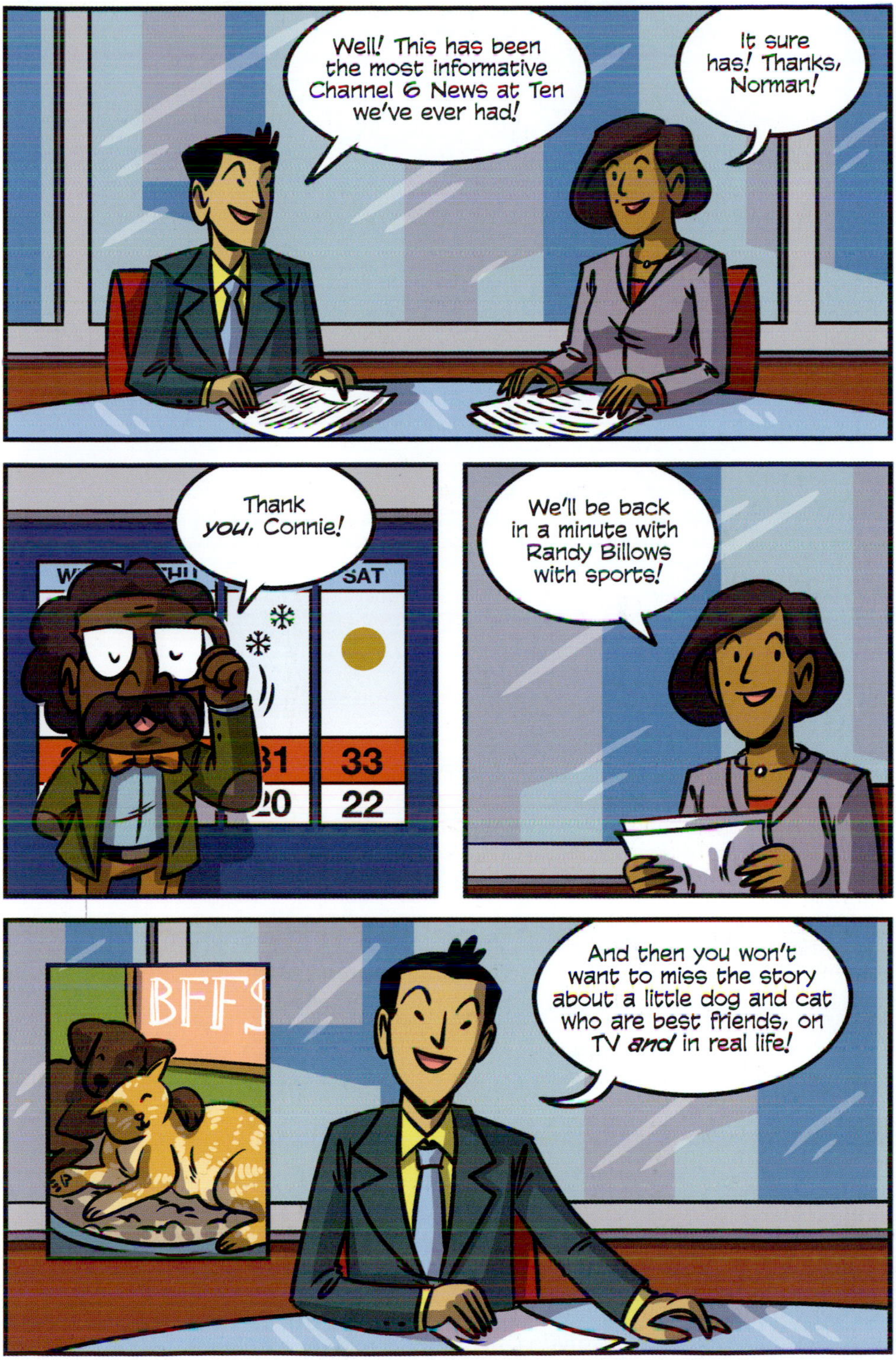
Well! This has been the most informative Channel 6 News at Ten we've ever had!
It sure has! Thanks, Norman!
Thank *you*, Connie!
SAT
33
22
We'll be back in a minute with Randy Billows with sports!
And then you won't want to miss the story about a little dog and cat who are best friends, on TV *and* in real life!

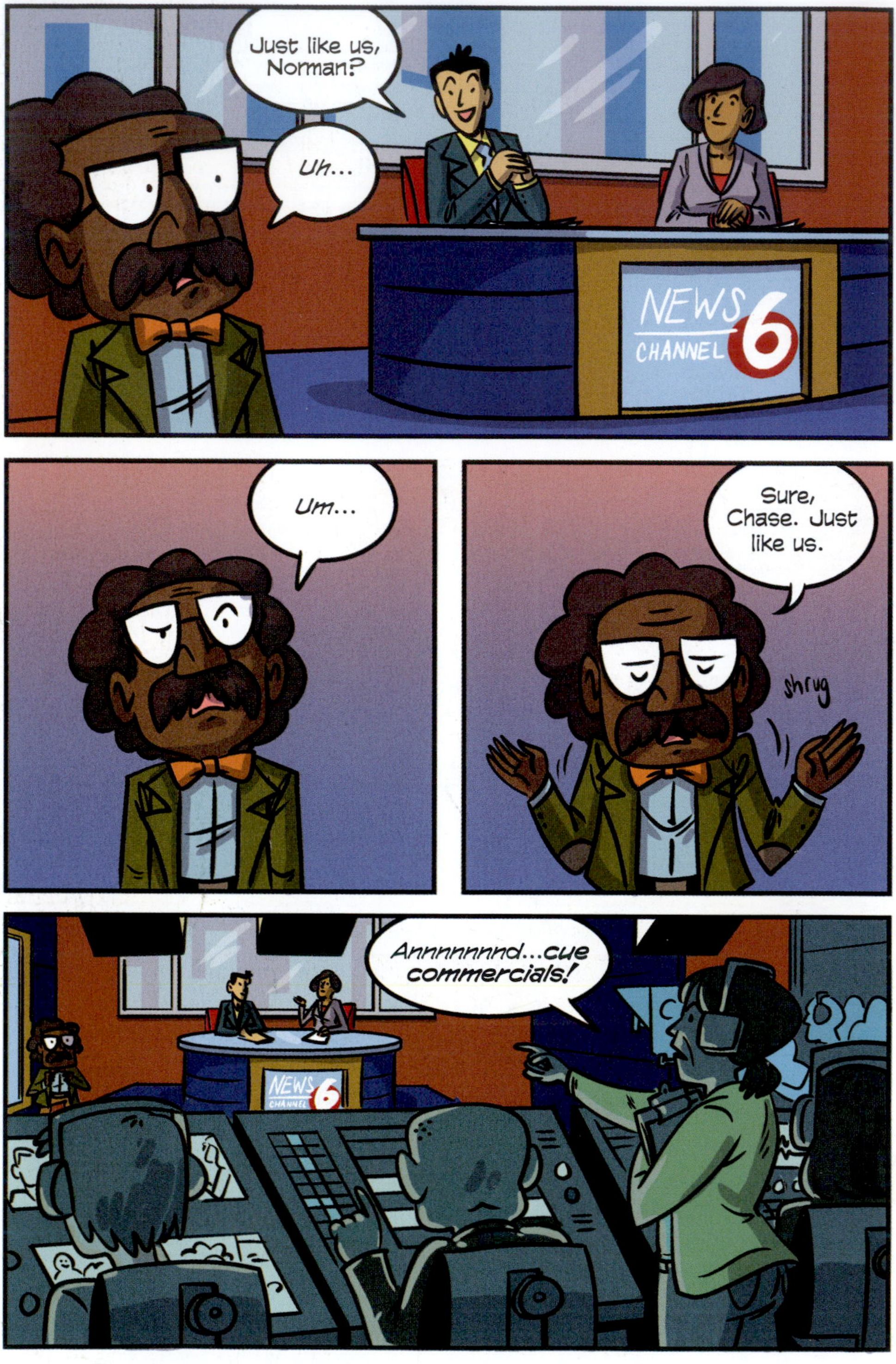
Just like us, Norman?
Uh...
Um...
Sure, Chase. Just like us.
shrug
Annnnnnnd...cue commercials!
NEWS CHANNEL 6

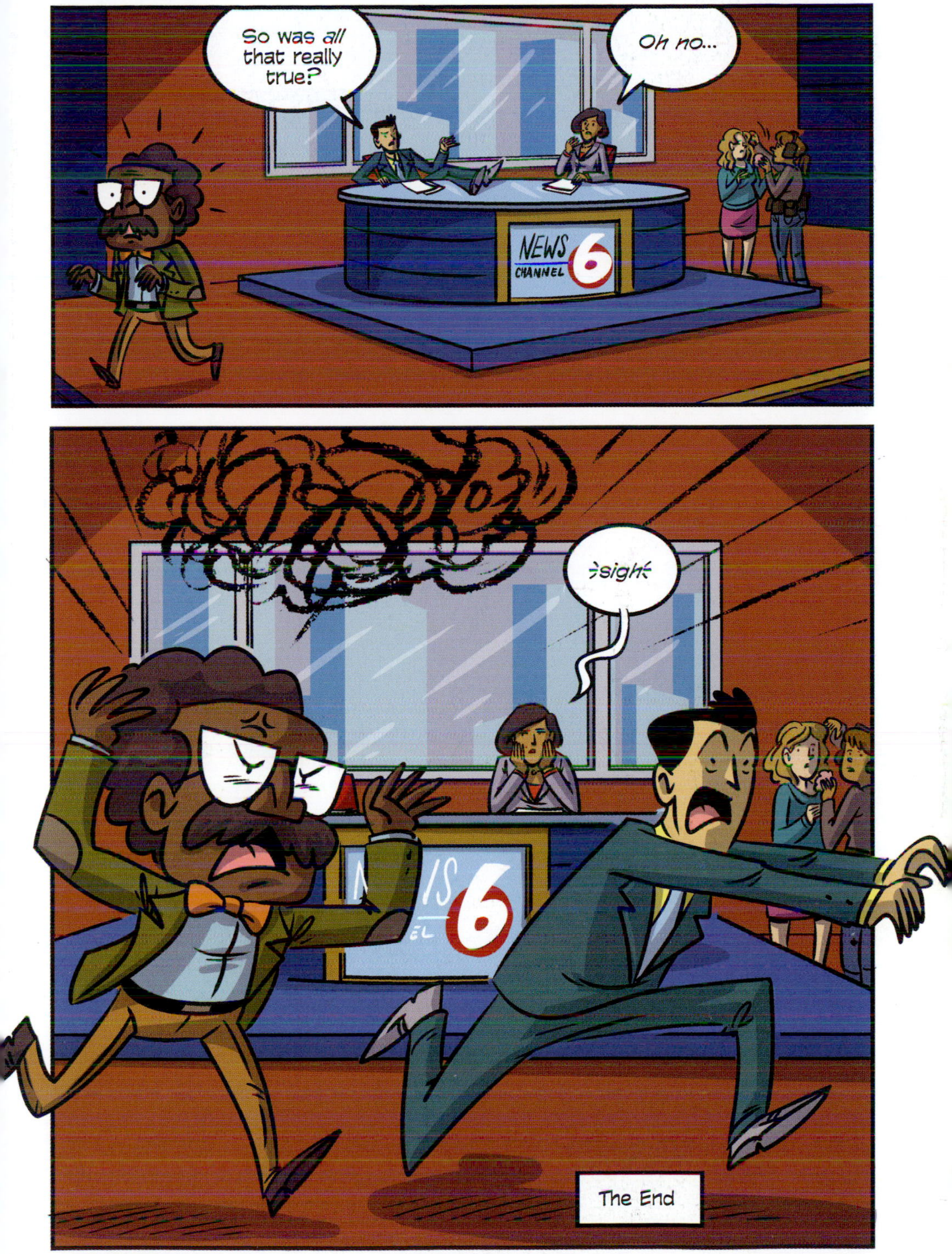
So was *all* that really true?
Oh no...
sigh
The End

—GLOSSARY—

Atmosphere

The layers of gas surrounding a planet between the surface and outer space.

Axis

An imaginary line on which a sphere rotates.

Carbon footprint

The amount of carbon dioxide or carbon compounds emitted due to the fossil fuels made in the production of materials used by a person or group.

Circulation

The movement of a fluid or gas within a contained space or back and forth around an area.

Celsius

The standard scientific unit of measurement for temperature.

Climate

The general weather conditions in an area over a period of time.

Condensation

When a vapor or gas becomes a liquid.

Crystallize

When a substance hardens into a rigid solid form.

Drought

A period of time without rain that is longer than average for an area.

Ecosystem

A community of interacting organisms and their environment.

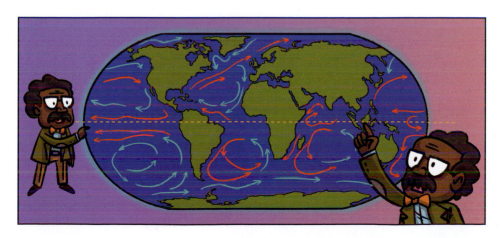

—GLOSSARY CONTINUED—

Environment
The surroundings that a person or living thing exist in.

Erosion
Gradually wearing away or destroying something over a length of time.

Evaporation
The process through which liquid water becomes a gas.

Fahrenheit
The US standard unit of measurement for temperature.

Floodplain
An area where flooding regularly occurs.

Granules
Small units of substance, such as grains.

Hemisphere
One half of a sphere, or one half of the planet.

Meteorology
The study of weather.

Polar
Having to do with the North or South Pole.

Precipitation
Moisture condensed from water vapor, which falls to the earth.

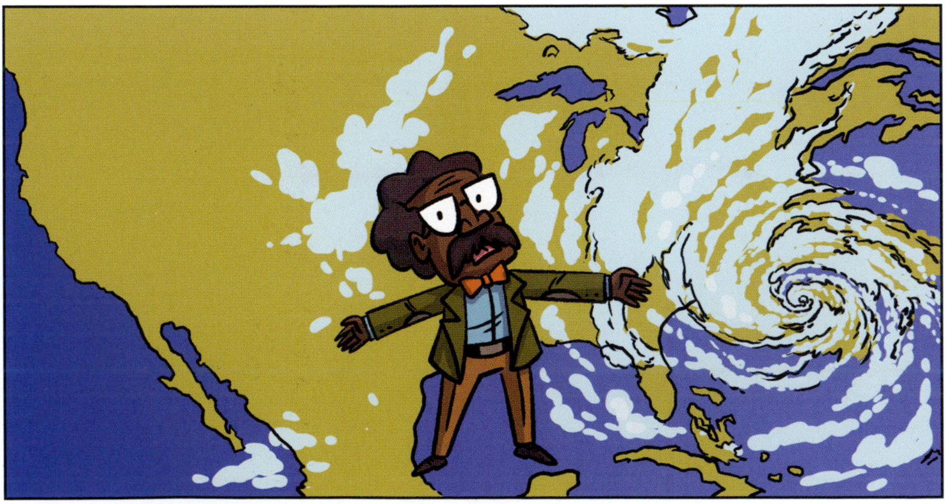

Rotate

To move in a set path around an axis, to revolve.

Sphere

Shaped like a round ball.

Thermometer

A device that measures temperature.

Transpiration

The process through which a plant releases water vapor.

Updraft

An upward current of air.

Urban

Relating to a city.

Vapor

A substance diffused in the air or a gas.

Virga

Rain that evaporates before it hits the ground.

Watershed

An area of land that drains streams and rainfall to a common outlet such as a reservoir, basin, or mouth of a bay.

Weather

The daily conditions of the atmosphere, regarding heat, humidity, wind, precipitation, and cloud conditions.

—WEATHER TOOLS—

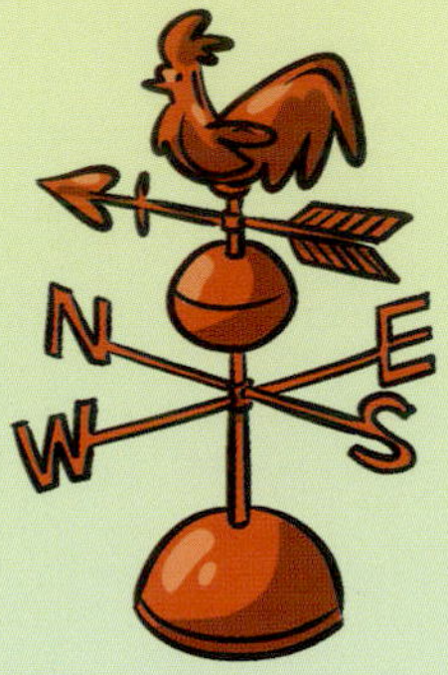
N
E
W
S

Wind vane—points in the direction the wind is blowing from

Anemometer—tells how fast the wind is blowing

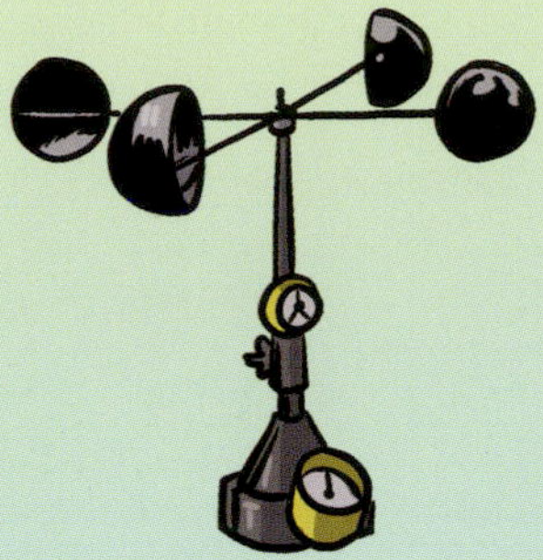

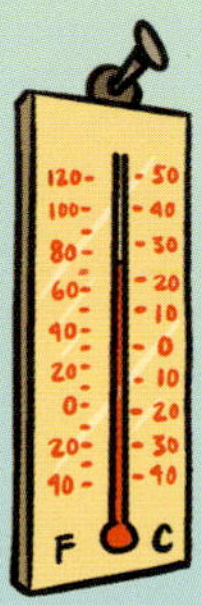
F
C

Thermometer—an instrument that measures the temperature

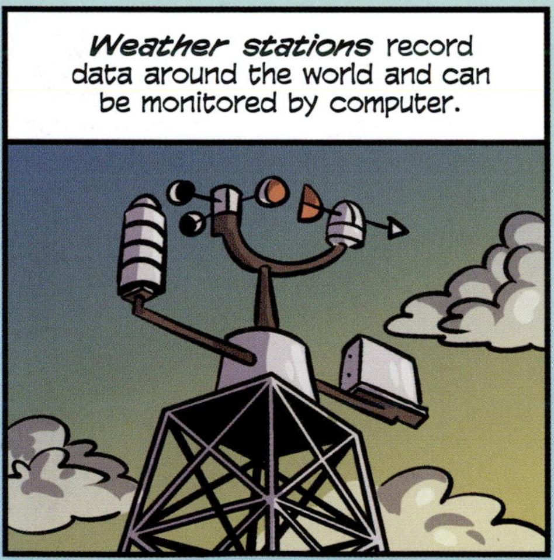
Weather stations record data around the world and can be monitored by computer.

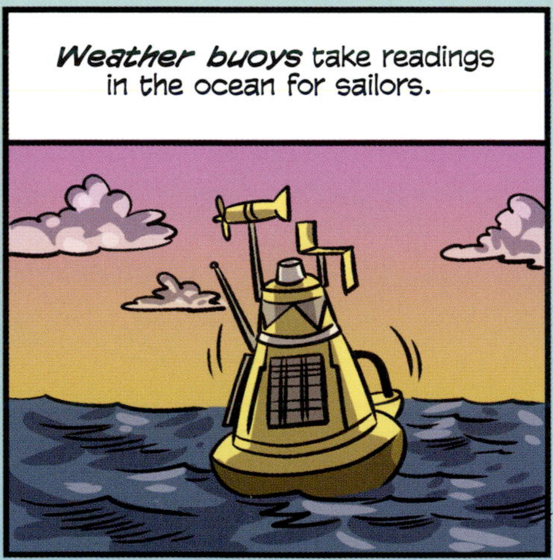
Weather buoys take readings in the ocean for sailors.

Hygrometer—an instrument that measures the water vapor content of the atmosphere
NORMAL
VERY DRY
Rain gauge—collects the rain and tells how much has fallen at a certain location
Barometer—measures the atmospheric pressure
BAROMETER
Radar can show us what's happening in the clouds.
Satellites can take readings from space on temperature, wind, and humidity, and give us details about clouds and their movements.

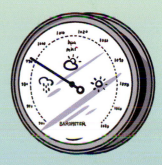

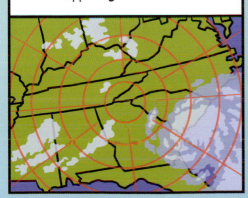

—WILD WEATHER MYTHS: DEBUNKED!—

by Alicia Wasula, consulting meteorologist

Is the air really "too heavy" to hit home runs on humid days?

No! Humid air contains a lot of water vapor, which is less dense than some of the other gasses in the atmosphere. So actually, it is theoretically possible to hit more home runs on humid days than on dry days. However, elevation matters too. Ball parks at high altitudes with thinner atmosphere, such as Coors Field, where the Colorado Rockies play, see more home runs hit than at other ball parks.

Is a car a safe place to be during a thunderstorm?

Yes, but maybe not for the reason you might expect. Many people learn that the rubber in the tires acts as an insulation against lightning striking the car. In fact, the metal frame of the car acts like what is known as a "Faraday cage," essentially keeping all of the electrical current on the outside of the car. So as long as you're not touching metal parts of the frame, you are safe from lightning strikes inside your car.

Do "pure" raindrops exist?

No! Every cloud and raindrop forms on a surface, known as a nucleus. Nuclei can be tiny solid particles such as dust, sea salt, sand, or even tiny bugs!

Does the cone of uncertainty represent the size of the hurricane?

No! The "cone of uncertainty" forecast, like the one shown for Hurricane Maria (2017) here, represents the range of potential tracks that the storm center may follow. The further out the forecast is in time, the wider the cone, or the larger the range in possible tracks. It is possible to experience effects of the storm even outside of the cone because a hurricane's effects can extend out from the center of the track.

35 N
30 N
25 N
20 N
15 N
10 N
2 PM Sat
2 PM Fri
2 AM Wed
5 PM Mon
2 PM Thu
2 PM Wed
2 PM Tue
90 W
85 W
80 W
75 W
70 W
65 W
60 W
55 W
50 W
45 W

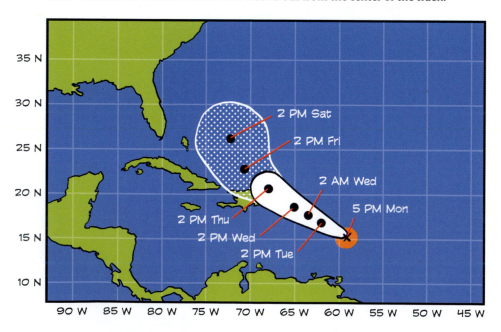

Should I open my windows during a tornado to equalize the pressure inside my house?

Absolutely not! By opening your windows during a tornado or other windstorm, you allow flying debris to enter your house and potentially injure the people inside. During a tornado, the safest place to be is in a windowless room toward the interior of the house.

Can cows predict rain?

Maybe, but it is hard to tell for sure because cows lie down for many reasons (like people!) and they cannot tell us why.

Are double rainbows identical to each other?

When you see a double rainbow, the inner rainbow has the more common color arrangement of red on the outside, orange, yellow, green, blue, and violet on the inside. In the less commonly seen outer arc, the colors are in reverse order so that violet will appear on the outside of the rainbow!

My soccer coach said that it is more dangerous to play in a dry heat than in a humid heat. Is this correct?

Your coach is right! On a dry day, your sweat evaporates much more readily from your skin than on a humid day, so it is possible to lose more fluids if you don't drink enough. However, on a humid day your sweat doesn't evaporate as efficiently, so it is still possible to overheat. The bottom line: if it's a hot day, make sure to hydrate well and take breaks if you are outside.

—WILD WEATHER MYTHS: CONTINUED!—

My dad put salt on our icy driveway and told me that it would melt the ice. How does this happen?

Actually, salt does not technically "melt" ice. When put on icy pavement, salt slowly dissolves into the ice, creating a salty solution. The freezing point of salt water is lower than the freezing point of plain water (32 degrees Fahrenheit), and so the ice that would have been frozen at 32 degrees can remain liquid at much colder temperatures than if no salt had been used.

Can lightning strike the same place twice?

Although popular belief would say that "lightning can't strike the same place twice," this is really not true. Tall locations are particularly prone to repeated lightning strikes. The Empire State Building, in New York City, has been struck by lightning many times over the years!

Do raindrops really look like teardrops when they fall?

Surprisingly, this is not the most aerodynamic shape that liquid raindrops take when they fall down to the ground. As a drop falls, the air resistance pushes upward on the center of the drop, which then assumes a hamburger-bun-like shape. Eventually the force becomes large enough that the drop can break apart into smaller drops, and the process repeats.

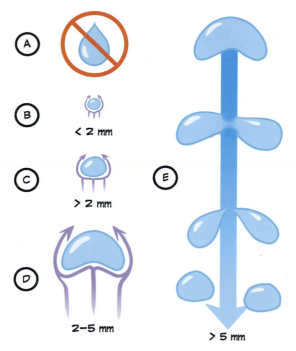

Different sizes of raindrops:

A) Raindrops are not tear-shaped, as most people think.

B) Very small raindrops are almost spherical in shape.

C) Larger raindrops become flattened at the bottom, like that of a hamburger bun, due to air resistance.

D) Large raindrops have a large amount of air resistance, which makes them begin to become unstable.

E) Very large raindrops split into smaller raindrops due to air resistance.

A

B < 2 mm

C > 2 mm

E

D 2–5 mm

> 5 mm

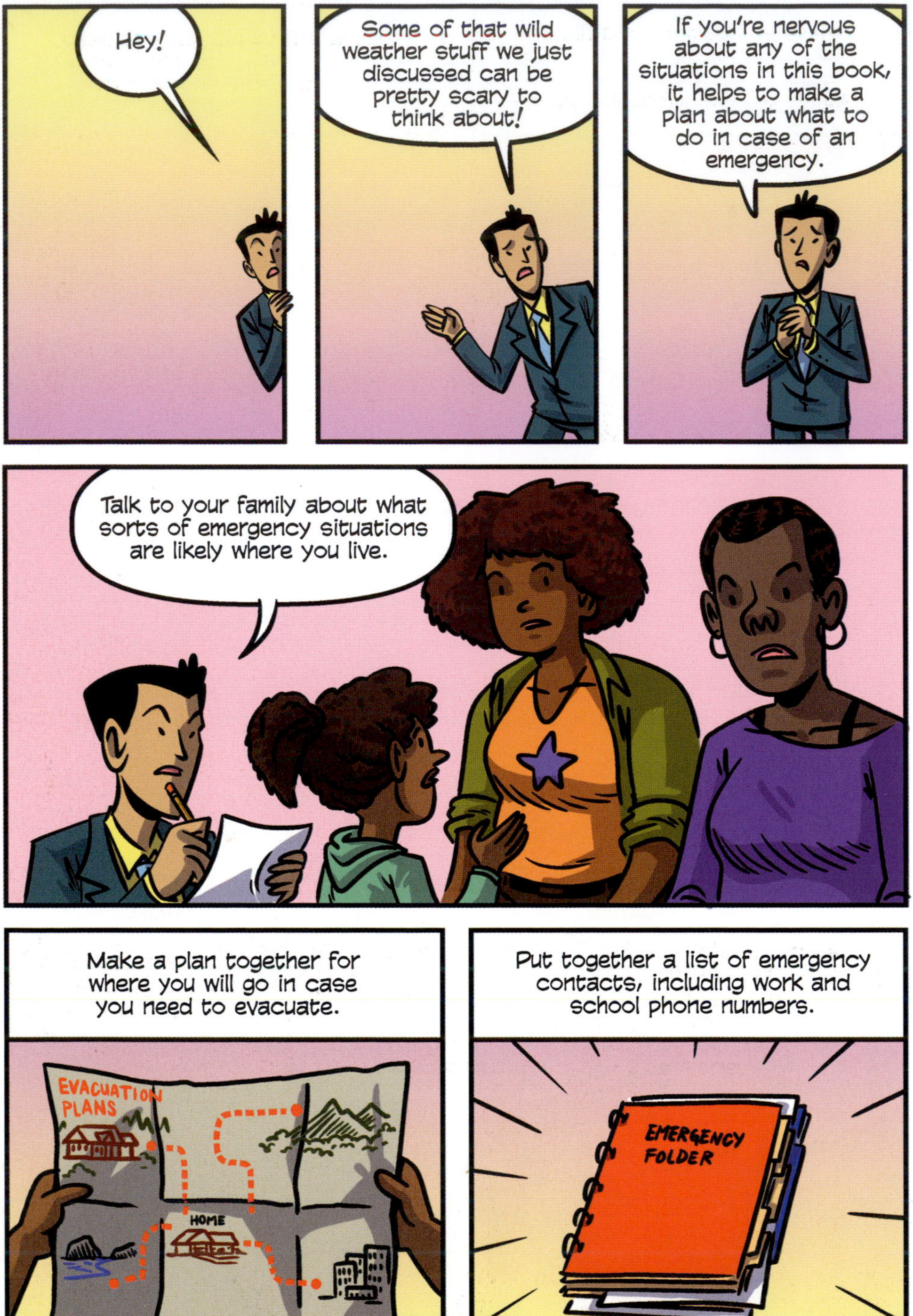
Hey!
Some of that wild weather stuff we just discussed can be pretty scary to think about!
If you're nervous about any of the situations in this book, it helps to make a plan about what to do in case of an emergency.
Talk to your family about what sorts of emergency situations are likely where you live.
Make a plan together for where you will go in case you need to evacuate.
EVACUATION PLANS
HOME
Put together a list of emergency contacts, including work and school phone numbers.
EMERGENCY FOLDER

Have an adult make a file of important information like bank account numbers, insurance policies, and identification papers.

Have a first aid kit, and keep some nonperishable food and extra bottled water in your home.

Finally, make a packing list of necessities you'll need to pack, like diapers, pet supplies, medicine, and dietary considerations to prepare for.

Ready.gov has guidelines for all kinds of disasters, like fires, droughts, tornadoes, tsunamis, hurricanes, and even super-rare stuff like SPACE WEATHER!

www.ready.gov

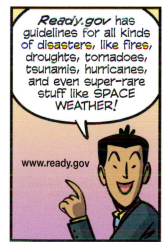

You can talk with your family about what to do in those circumstances and have a plan so you'll all be safe.

Phew! I already feel more relaxed just talking about it.

GET TO KNOW YOUR UNIVERSE!
SCIENCE COMICS
"An excellent addition to school and classroom libraries."
—School Library Journal
CORAL REEFS
Cities of the Ocean
MARIS WICKS
DINOSAURS
Fossils and Feathers
MK REED JOE FLOOD
VOLCANOES
Fire and Life
JON CHAD
BATS
Learning to Fly
FALYNN KOCH
FLYING MACHINES
How the Wright Brothers Soared
ALISON WILGUS MOLLY BROOKS
PLAGUES
The Microscopic Battlefield
FALYNN KOCH
DOGS
From Predator to Protector
ANDY HIRSCH
ROBOTS AND DRONES
Past, Present, and Future
MAIRGHREAD SCOTT JACOB CHABOT
SHARKS
Nature's Perfect Hunter
JOE FLOOD
ROCKETS
Defying Gravity
ANNE DROZD JERZY DROZD
TREES
Kings of the Forest
ANDY HIRSCH
THE BRAIN
The Ultimate Thinking Machine
TORY WOOLLCOTT ALEX GRAUDINS
SOLAR SYSTEM
Our Place in Space
ROSEMARY MOSCO JON CHAD
POLAR BEARS
Survival on the Ice
JASON VIOLA ZACK GIALLONGO
...And more books coming soon!

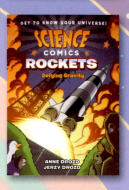

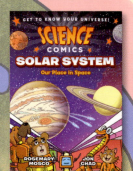